Get On Up With Java

Rich Picking

Lexden Publishing
www.lexden-publishing.co.uk

Acknowledgements

This book has been developed over a number of years from lectures, lab exercises, and tutorials. I owe much gratitude to the students and academic staff who have provided input and feedback during this time. In particular I would like to thank Ken Croston, Stuart Cunningham, John Davies, Mark Kench, Mike Morgan, and Inge Powell.

Rich Picking
Wrexham, July 2007

First published in 2007 by Lexden Publishing Ltd.

British Library Cataloguing in Publication Data
A CIP record for this book is available from the British Library.

ISBN: 978 1 904995 18 0
e-Book ISBN: 978 1 904995 28 9

Printed by Lightning Source

Lexden Publishing Ltd
23 Irvine Road
Colchester
Essex
C03 3TS

Tel: 01206 533164
Email: **info@lexden-publishing.co.uk**
www.lexden-publishing.co.uk

CONTENTS

FOREWORD

For the student

If you want to learn how to solve problems, and program their solutions in Java, this book is for you.

Java is well-established as the language of choice for the Internet and for many other applications. It is also popular for mobile phone technologies and for other everyday computer-controlled devices. Take a look in a modern kitchen for example – one of your appliances has probably got a Java program in it somewhere.

This book makes no assumptions about your programming experience. Consequently, it starts from the utmost basics. If you do have some prior knowledge of programming, whether a little Java or maybe other languages, you can always skip over the early chapters.

You may have access to Java in your school, college or university, but it's well worth getting your own copy so you can work with greater flexibility. The good news is that Java is completely free. However, it can be a bit of a pain to get up and running so a simple step-by-step guide to help you through this initial phase has been provided (*see page 6*). This installation guide is for PC users only, so if you are using an Apple or a UNIX-based machine, you'll have to rely on other resources to help you instead. Java's official website, **http://java.sun.com**, is a good place to start.

For the lecturer

This book is intended for students new to *structured* programming and is suitable for entry level courses in computing.

Throughout this text, students are encouraged to design their programs using a structured, top-down approach prior to coding and testing them.

The method used in this book maps the layout of graphical charting directly onto that of the code layout.

It uses completely different shaped boxes to signify sequence, selection and iteration. This method greatly improves the accuracy and quality of design charts. On *page 4* is a simple example – you can see that the physical mapping between the design chart and the code layout is patently clear.

This technique encourages students to adopt another good practice that is often lacking – indentation!

Design, write and test a program to input student marks in a test. Output 'Pass' if the mark is 40 or above, otherwise output 'Fail'. Input a mark of -1 to finish the program.

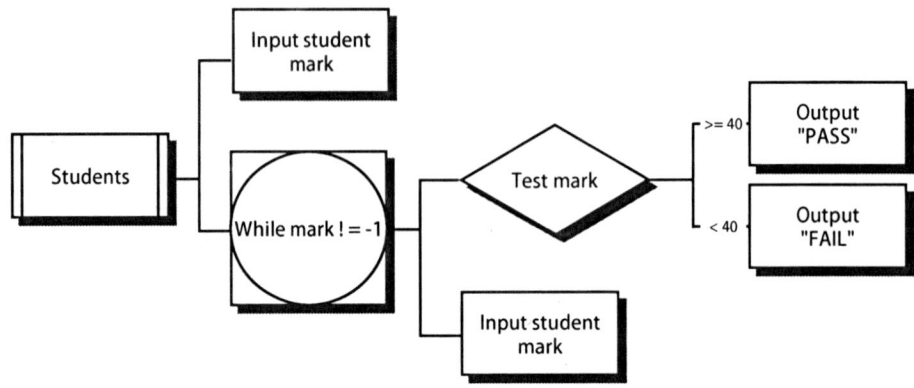

```java
import java.util.Scanner;

/*
This program asks the user to input student marks in a test.
Output 'Pass' if the mark is 40 or above, otherwise output
'Fail'.
Input a mark of -1 to finish the program.
*/
class Students
{
    public static void main (String [] args)
    {
        Scanner input = new Scanner(System.in);

        int mark;

        // READ AHEAD of the 'while' test!!!
        System.out.print("Please input mark (-1 to finish) ");
        mark = input.nextInt();

        while (mark != -1)
        {
            if (mark >= 40)
                    System.out.println("Pass");
            else
                    System.out.println("Fail");

            /* READ AHEAD of the 'while' test, otherwise you
            can't get out the loop!!! */
            System.out.print("Please input mark (-1 to
            finish) ");
            mark = input.nextInt();
        }

    }
}
```

Towards the end of the book, object-oriented programming is introduced. The principles of classes, objects, encapsulation and inheritance are explained – polymorphism is beyond the scope of this text.

A highly simplified UML notation to help students understand basic class architectures has been used.

The version of Java required for this book is **JDK v.1.5 or later**. This is because the Scanner class is used throughout to simplify user input. All programs run in the console (command) window, except for the example at the end of the book, which gives students some insight into how they can develop their skills in applet programming, once they have gained the fundamentals described in this introductory text.

HOW TO INSTALL JAVA

As you are going to download a large installation file from Java's official website it would be useful to have a broadband connection.

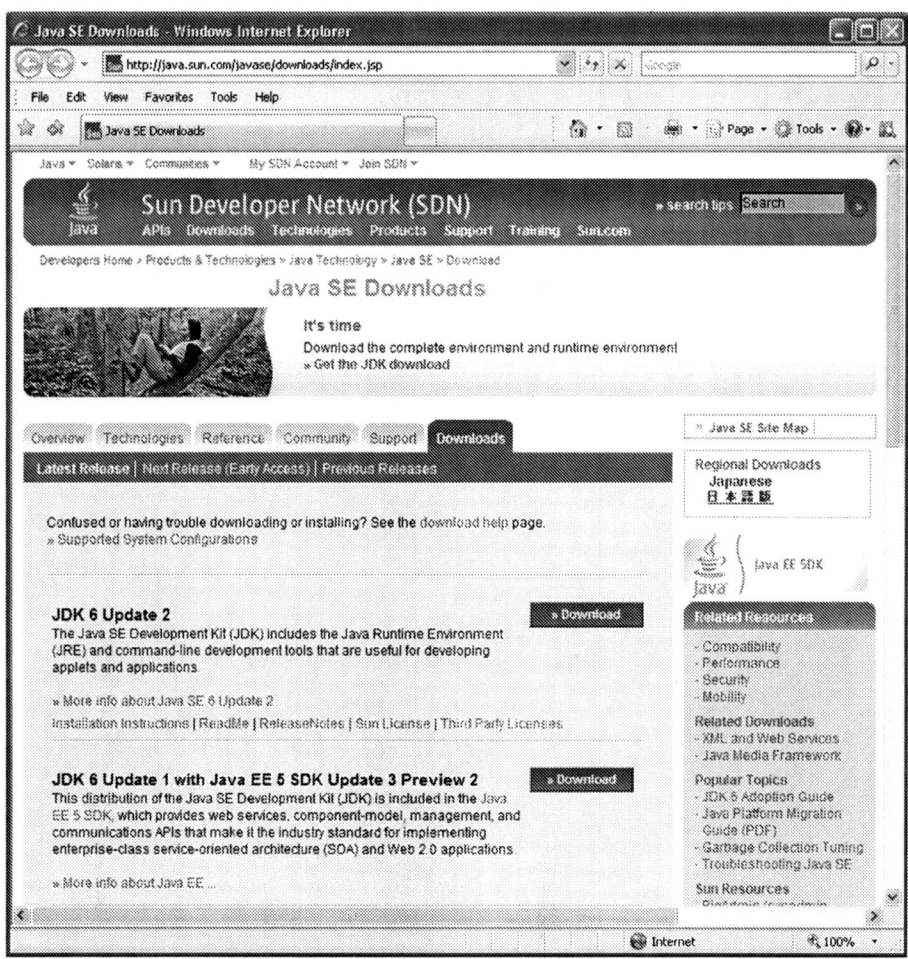

Launch your web browser.

Go to **http://java.sun.com/javase/downloads**.

You should see a page with a list of downloadable releases of Java:

The latest version is always the first download in the list – at this time it is called JDK 6 Update 2.

Click on the **Download** button which will take you to the next page:

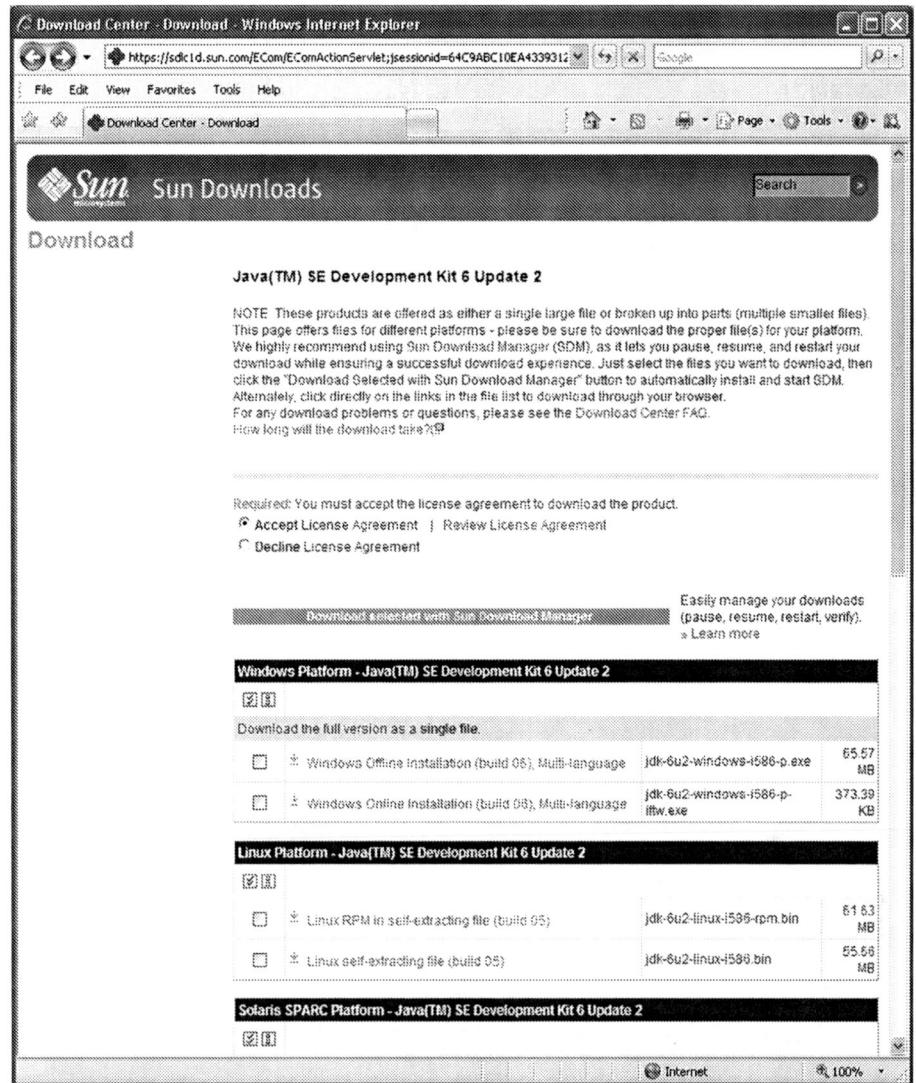

Accept the **License Agreement**.

Select one of the **Windows Platform** options. You don't need to check the box on the left-hand side – simply click the blue text. The first option **Windows Offline Installation** is the smallest file to download, so it makes sense to click on that one.

Next, you'll be given the option to download the installation file to your PC.

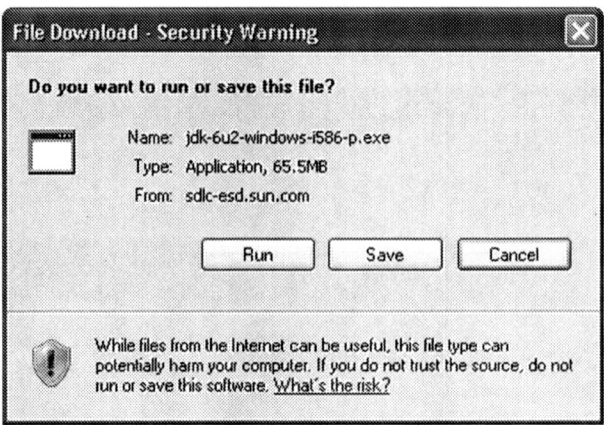

 Click on the **Save** button.

This will save the file to your desktop by default, but you have the option to select a different location if you wish.

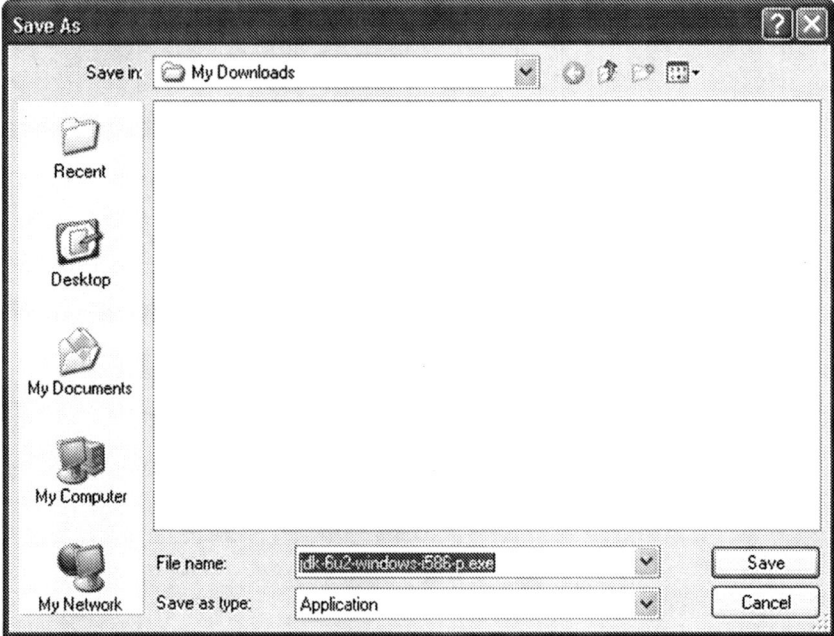

Once you've downloaded the installation file, locate the folder where you downloaded it to.

 Double-click on the file.

A wizard is then launched that will take you through a simple installation process. Once you've successfully gone through this, you should finally get a message like this:

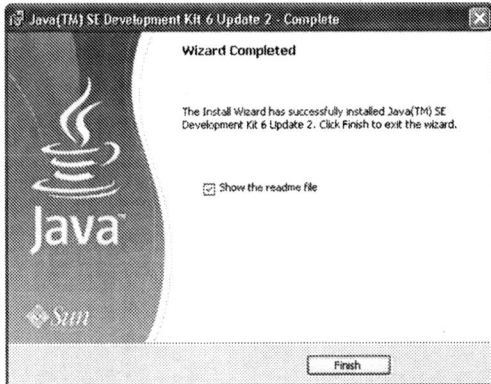

 Select the **Finish** button.

Although Java has now been installed there are still a few more steps to go through before you can start programming.

 Go to the location where you have installed Java and check that there are two new folders in that location. If you followed the default installation sequence, they'll be in **C:\Program Files\Java**.

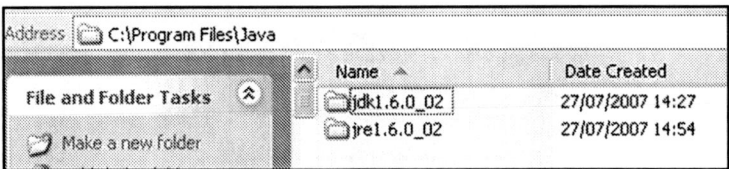

You'll need to set up the **path** on your computer, so that Java can fully function properly. To do this:

 Go to your **Control Panel** (accessed from the Windows **Start Menu**).

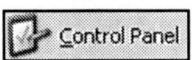

 Double-click on the **System** icon.

System

The **Systems Properties** window will be displayed.

 Select the **Advanced** tab.

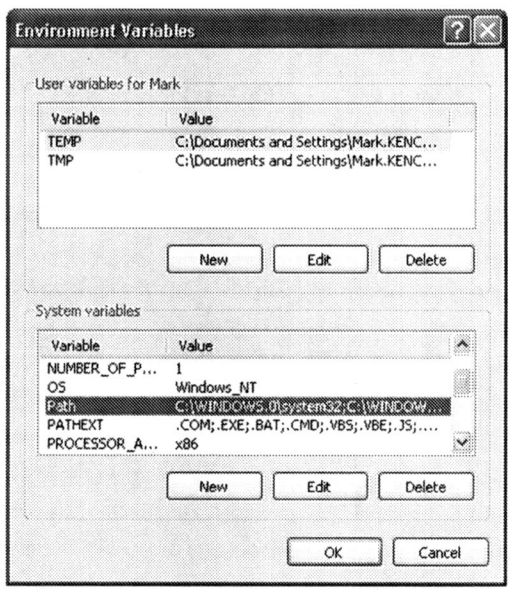

Select the **Environment Variables** button.

You should now see two panes in the **Environment Variables** window.

Scroll in the **System Variables** list until you see the **Path** entry.

Select this, and click **Edit**.

The **Edit System Variable** window will be displayed (*see below*). This contains path information for, possibly, a number of applications and may be very long. We need to add path information at the end of this for Java to work.

 Click in the **Variable value** field.

 Move your cursor to the very end of the text displayed in this filed by pressing the **End** key on your keyboard.

You should now see the cursor flashing at the end of the text.

 Type a *semi-colon (;)*, followed by the full path of the location of your Java installation. For our installation to work we typed in:
  ;C:\Program Files\Java\jdk1.6.0_02\bin (*see below*).

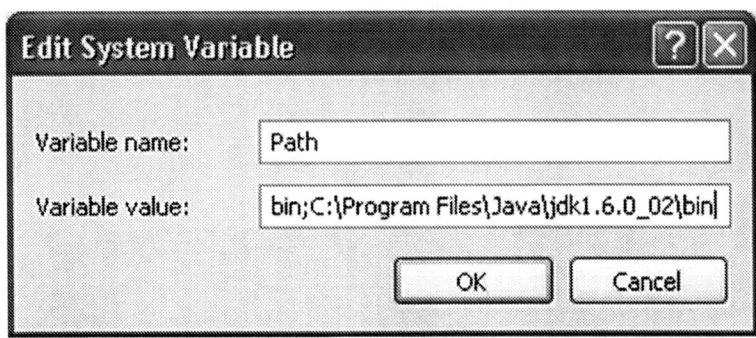

Notice that the **jdk** folder and the word **bin** is also included in this. Make sure each folder in this path list is separated by a backslash, and that it is **EXACTLY** as you saw it when you checked the location of your installation. Once you are entirely confident about this, click **OK** in each panel and close the **Control Panel** window.

To check that everything is working now in preparation for your first Java program, you'll need to launch a **Command window**.

NOTE

You'll need to launch a **Command window** for all your Java programming throughout this book.

To do this:

 Click on the **Start Menu**

 Select **Run**.

 In the **Run** window type **cmd**.

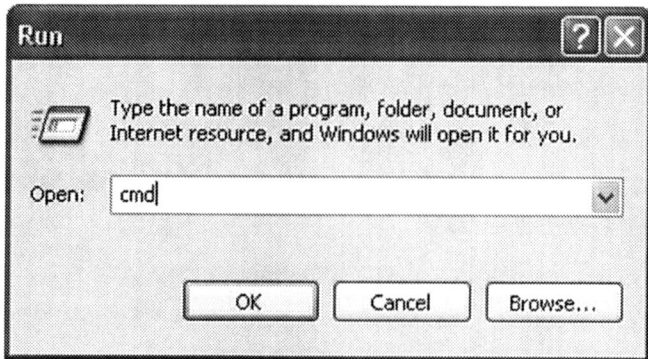

A DOS window similar to the one shown below should be displayed.

▶ Type **java –version**.

▶ Press either the **Return** or **Enter** key.

If you have set your path correctly, you should see a message that tells you there is a recognized version of Java installed on your machine, like this:

```
C:\WINDOWS\system32\cmd.exe

Microsoft Windows XP [Version 5.1.2600]
(C) Copyright 1985-2001 Microsoft Corp.

C:\>java -version
java version "1.6.0_02"
Java(TM) SE Runtime Environment (build 1.6.0_02-b06)
Java HotSpot(TM) Client VM (build 1.6.0_02-b06, mixed mode, sharing)

C:\>_
```

Congratulations – you have now installed Java.

EXPERT ADVICE

It is a good idea to store all the Java programs you are going to create in a common location. If you create a folder called Java, and store them all there, whenever you run your programs in future you will be able to access this folder from the **Command window**, simply by typing **cd Java**.

Happy programming!!

Chapter 1

GETTING STARTED

Chapter overview

The aim of this chapter is just as it says – to get you started. It is very important to note that you are not expected to understand everything you do at this stage.

At the end of this chapter you will be able to:

 write your first Java programs;

 run Java computer programs;

 create a template to help you write future programs.

Computer programs

A **computer program** is a set of instructions we give to a computer. There are many examples of sets of instructions we see in our everyday lives. Most of them are meant for people to follow, such as directions to a destination, or a recipe for a dinner. The computer can also follow a set of instructions. We write those instructions in a special format called a computer program.

The computer follows these instructions to do a job for us. As we all know, computers are very powerful devices. They can perform mathematical calculations very accurately and quickly. They can format documents and presentations in a professional and consistent manner. They can process lots of information and display it in many ways on a computer screen – they do this when we play computer games, for example.

When the computer carries out a job for us, it is called **running** a program. Not so long ago, computer programs *ran* from tape machines. The instructions were stored on magnetic tapes, which were run across a tape head reader to extract the data into the computer system. Nowadays, we use faster, more sophisticated storage devices, such as magnetic disks and optical devices (such as compact discs) to store our programs and data.

We have to instruct the computer using a language it can understand. When we write our computer programs, we need to use a specially designed set of instructions which the computer can interpret, and translate into the basic language of computers, called **machine code**. Machine code is very simple – it consists of huge sequences of **ons** and **offs**, or **ones** and **zeros**.

To write the most trivial of computer programs requires millions and millions of **ones** and **zeros**. Obviously, we don't want to have to do this. It would be too difficult and too time consuming to instruct the computer in such a way. Rather, we tend to write instructions in a language more akin to our own. This language is called a **computer programming language**.

The words in the language are called **code**. You will see as we write our programs, that the code follows very strict rules of spelling and grammar. We tend to use the word **syntax** to describe the rules that govern the code of the language. When we write our computer programs, we have to go through a process (called **compilation**) where the computer tries to translate the code we have written into machine code, and that the rules have been properly adhered to. If there are problems, the computer lets us know, and won't run the program. We then have to rectify the problems, and go through the process again. A special computer program carries out the process – it's called a **compiler**.

There are many programming languages. Some have been developed for specific jobs, some are based on differing structures and even philosophies. For example, there is a language called **FORTRAN**, which was developed for *number-crunching* and engineering programs. Another, known as **COBOL**, was developed for business and banking applications. Both these languages were developed in the 1960s, and to a certain extent have been superseded by newer, faster, and more sophisticated variants. In this book, we will use **Java**. Java is a relatively new language. It is very powerful and can be used on many different types of computer. Because it is so versatile, it is very popular for Internet-based applications.

Here is our first Java program. It doesn't matter at this stage if you do not understand what it means. This will come later.

Your first program

> **EXPERT ADVICE**
>
> It is a good idea to store all the Java programs you are going to create in a common location. If you create a folder called **Java**, and store them all there, whenever you run your programs in future you will be able to access this folder from the **Command Window**, simply by typing **cd Java**.

```
/* This program says Hello */
class Hello
{
   public static void main(String[] args)
   {
       System.out.print("Hello");
   }
}
```

 Carefully type in the example computer program above using a simple text editor (e.g. **Notepad**).

> **EXPERT ADVICE**
>
> Make sure you use **upper case** (capital letters) and **lower case** (small letters) exactly as you see it. Java is **case-sensitive**.

▶ Save the file into your **Java** folder and call it **Hello.java**.

▶ Open a **Command prompt window** (*see page 11*).

▶ Type **javac Hello.java**.

▶ Press the **Enter** key.

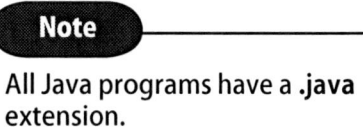

Note

All Java programs have a **.java** extension.

```
C:\WINDOWS\system32\cmd.exe

Microsoft Windows XP [Version 5.1.2600]
(C) Copyright 1985-2001 Microsoft Corp.

C:\>cd java

C:\Java>javac Hello.java

C:\Java>
```

The command **javac** means **java compile**. It starts a process called **compilation** and uses Java's own **compiler** to do this work.

The compiler will take a few seconds to try to convert your program into a form it can work with and when it is ready the Java directory will be displayed (**C:\Java>**).

If the compiler has not understood your instructions, it will give you a message explaining why. If you get such a message then you should carefully check that your typing matches exactly that of the program on *page 14*. If there are problems, you'll need to modify your program, save it, and compile it again. You may need to go through these steps several times before you get the program exactly right.

Once everything is OK, you won't get a message. You should now have a new file in your Java folder called **Hello.class**. This is called a **class file** and it was produced by the compiler. This means that the compiler is 'happy' with the code so you can now go on to run the program.

▶ In the **Command window**, type **java Hello**.

▶ Press the **Enter** key.

Your program should now run and display the word **Hello** on the next line in the **Command prompt window**.

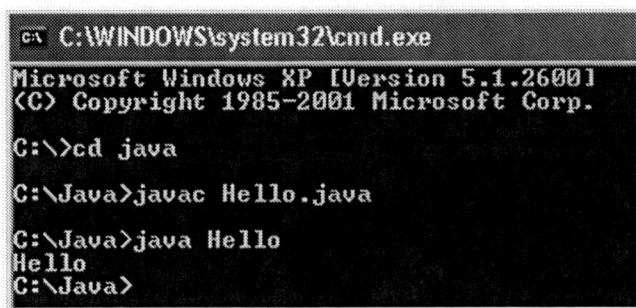

```
C:\WINDOWS\system32\cmd.exe

Microsoft Windows XP [Version 5.1.2600]
(C) Copyright 1985-2001 Microsoft Corp.

C:\>cd java

C:\Java>javac Hello.java

C:\Java>java Hello
Hello
C:\Java>
```

If you do not see the word **Hello** appear, there may still be a problem with your program. Check your code again.

Our first program is very short and very simple. All it does is display a message – **Hello** (notice that, in the program code the message is placed in double quotes).

Exercise 1.1: Hello, how are you?

 Modify your program so that the message "Hello, how are you today?" is displayed.

Your program should look almost identical to your first program. You only need to modify one line.

 Compile and run your program.

In any language, spoken or computer, there are certain rules to follow so that things make sense. A computer programming language has very strict rules that we must follow, otherwise the computer won't understand our instructions. Contrary to popular belief, computers aren't 'clever'. In fact, they are quite 'stupid'. They only do what we tell them to do. The catch is though, that we have to tell them *exactly* what to do in a rather *formal* way. A computer cannot work out what we mean through reason or argument. It only follows the instructions we give it, and we must give it precise instructions in a very precise language. If there are any language errors in our program, it will not work. An error in a program is called a **bug**.

Writing in a programming language, such as Java, can be a very frustrating experience. One simple mistake can completely foul up the whole thing, for example missing a quote symbol, using lower case for one letter where upper is expected, getting a bracket in the wrong place, and so forth.

Whenever we face frustration, it's always a good idea to try to make things easier wherever possible. One thing we can do already at this early stage of our programming development is to identify code that is common to all the programs we will write. Here are some lines that will feature in just about every one of your Java programs from now on:

```
import java.util.Scanner;

/* This program … */
class ???
{
    public static void main(String[] args)
    {
    }
}
```

Exercise 1.2: Template

 Create a template that looks like the code on *page 16*. Save it as **Template.java**.

Every time you create a new program you can now open **Template.java**, and then save it as something more meaningful. For example, **Hello.java** is a good name for our first program because it reminds us what the program does. If the program was to display the message Goodbye, then calling it **Hello.java** wouldn't be such a good idea.

Now when you write a new program, you will only need to write new instructions inside the second set of curly brackets. You will also need to change the name of the program, which is written after the word class. It needs to be **EXACTLY** the same as the file name (without the **.java**, of course).

Program comments

Lines that look like this:

```
/* This program … */
```

are called **program comments**. Use the space between the **/*** and the ***/** to remind yourself, and others, what the program does. Comments can be used at any point in your code. *See also page 33.*

Exercise 1.3: Goodbye

In this exercise you will use your new template and modify the program's comment.

▶ Open up the **Template.java** program and save it as **Goodbye.java**.

▶ Change the class name to **Goodbye**.

▶ Add the line that displays a message, **"Goodbye cruel world."**

▶ Change the comment so that it is meaningful to the program.

▶ Compile and then run the program.

Your program should look something like this:

```java
import java.util.Scanner;

/* This program outputs a goodbye message */
class Goodbye
{
    public static void main(String[] args)
    {
        System.out.print("Goodbye cruel world.");
    }
}
```

Input/Output

So far, you have written some programs that display various messages. We call this display **output**.

For a program to be truly useful, it will need to **interact** with the real world. For example, when you play a computer game, you need to be able to **input** instructions to the computer (such as selecting a one or two player option), as well as displaying the messages and graphics. This interaction is called **input/output**, or **i/o** for short.

Here is our first program that combines input and output. It's called **Greetings**.

```
import java.util.Scanner;

/* This program generates a Greetings message */
class Greetings
{
   public static void main (String [] args)
   {
       Scanner input = new Scanner(System.in);

       String s;

       System.out.print("What's your name?");

       s = input.next();

       System.out.print("Greetings " + s);
   }
}
```

In this program, we have introduced a **string** of characters (a word, for example) and we have called it **s**. We did this by typing the program statement:

```
String s;
```

In the program, **s** is used to remember the contents of the string of characters we will type in when the program runs.

This is done in the program statement:

```
s = input.next();
```

When the program runs, the user (that's you at the moment) will be asked:

```
What's your name?
```

Whatever the user types will be remembered by **s**. We might think of **s** as a location in the computer's memory. So if the user types in the word **Fred**, then **s** will store the string: *Fred*.

Whenever we recall **s** from the computer's memory, it will produce the word **Fred**. So when the last line of the program runs before the program ends, it will output:

```
Greetings Fred
```

Exercise 1.4: Greetings

▶ Open up **Template.java** and add the line:

```
Scanner input = new Scanner(System.in);
```

to the program in the place indicated by the program above. Save **Template.java**. Your template program can now deal with input as well as output.

▶ Create the Greetings program and save it as **Greetings.java**.

▶ Get the program working.

▶ See if you can work out how to modify your program to display: "Greetings **your name**. How are you today?"

Processing data

All computer programs process data in some way. Usually this means taking some form of input, perhaps from a computer keyboard, manipulating that input in some way, and outputting the result of that manipulation, perhaps to a computer screen. This form of manipulation is called **data processing**.

The following example processes data by performing a simple calculation. It converts pounds to kilograms.

```
import java.util.Scanner;

/* This program asks the user to input a weight in pounds,
   converts it to kilos, and outputs the result */
class ConvertWeight
{
   public static void main (String [] args)
   {
       Scanner input = new Scanner(System.in);

       double pounds, kilos;

       System.out.print("Please input a weight in pounds ");
       pounds = input.nextDouble();

       kilos = pounds / 2.2;

       System.out.print(pounds + " pounds = " + kilos + "
       kilos.");
   }
}
```

To analyse what this program does, it would be easier to break it up into three components:

1. **Input**: where the user is asked to input some data.
2. **Process**: where that data is manipulated.
3. **Output**: where the result is output.

In the program, the **input** component looks like this:

```
System.out.print("Please input a weight in kilos ");

pounds = input.nextDouble();
```

The **process** component looks like this:

```
kilos = pounds / 2.2;
```

The output component looks like this

```
System.out.print(pounds + " pounds = " + kilos + " kilos.");
```

EXPERT GUIDANCE

It's important to note that virtually all computer programs follow this three component pattern in some way. Think about some computer programs you use: a video game, a website, a cash machine. Invariably, you input something (fire a missile, click a link, enter your PIN), the computer processes your input (the enemy is destroyed, the computer accesses a web page, your PIN is checked), and on the screen, the results of the processing are displayed.

Exercise 1.5: Conversion

 Open up **Template.java** and add the new lines in the program on *page 19*.

 Save it as **ConvertWeight.java**.

 Get the program working and test it with variable values until you are confident it works.

Java Forum

Post	**What do the curly brackets mean?** ⭐
Reply	Essentially, they mean **Begin** and **End**. The open curly bracket { begins a list of program statements and the close curly bracket } ends them. They are also commonly called **braces**, or **squigglies**. As your programs become more complex, you'll need to use them more and more. ☺
Post	**OK, that covers the curly brackets. What about all the other ones?** ⭐
Reply	Most computer programming languages make extensive use of brackets to show where things begin and end. **Round brackets ()** are used in Java to mark the beginning and ending of messages. For example, in one of your programs, you had this program statement: `System.out.print("Please input a weight in pounds ");` The round brackets contain a print message which is to be sent to the computer system's output. The message contains the string **"Please input a weight in pounds "**. Round brackets are also used in Java, just as they are used generally, for more complex mathematical expressions. They indicate the order in which things should be calculated. Consider the following (non-Java) examples: $$6 + 4 \div 2$$ $$(6 + 4) \div 2$$ The first example equals **8**, because **4÷2** is evaluated first, and is then added to **6**. The second example equals **5**, as we have used to round brackets to make sure the division comes after the addition. Java conforms to the basic power rules of mathematics, where multiplication and division are performed before addition and subtraction in a complex expression. You may also have noticed some square brackets in your program **[]**. For now, you will only need square brackets in the template of your program, so you don't need to know what they mean. This will be explained in a later chapter. ☺

Post	**What do the double quotes mean?** ★
Reply	When words are placed inside double quotes, it means that you literally want those words to be used by the program. They cannot change. Let's consider an example from one of your programs: ```System.out.print("Greetings " + s);``` In this program statement we will always output the word **Greetings**. In fact, to be accurate, we will output the word **Greetings** followed by a space, as there is a space before the close double quote symbol. After the **Greetings** message, we will output an additional message. The additional message corresponds to whatever **s** holds. The difference between each message is that **Greetings** never changes, whereas **s** may be different every time we run the program. ☺

Post	**So what exactly is s then?** ★
Reply	In the **Greetings** program, **s** is an object that holds a **variable** value. We use variables to refer to anything that might change each time a program is run. A variable is a fundamental part of virtually all programs. Most programs have several variables. They are stored in the computer's memory. The variables in the **convertWeight** program are **kilos** and **pounds**. We will look at variables in more detail in the next chapter. ☺

Post	**Why do I need to put a semi-colon at the end of every line?** ★
Reply	The answer to this is that you don't. However, you do need to put a semi-colon (;) at the end of many program statements. For now, assume that you need to do this in every line with the following two exceptions: • where the *next line* has an open curly bracket; • where the *current line* is an open or close curly bracket. ☺

That ends the first chapter. You probably have many more questions at this stage. Hopefully, these will be answered in the next chapters.

Chapter 2

THE BRICKS AND MORTAR OF A PROGRAM

Chapter overview

Building a program is very much like building a house. You need the bricks and mortar, as well as other basic building materials. In this chapter, we will introduce the basic building materials used in the Java programming language. Of course, you've already used some of these in your early programs.

At the end of this chapter you will be able to:

- select appropriate features of the Java language to perform simple operations;
- understand the rudiments of building computer programs;
- appreciate the different components of computer programs.

The basic materials of computer programs

To introduce the building materials, we can describe them using four categories:

1. Operators
2. Keywords
3. Data
4. Control structures

We will look at the first three now, using examples to explain their use. Control structures are more complex, and are covered in *Chapters 3, 4* and *5*.

Operators

Operators are simple tools that allow us to manipulate data. If you look at an electronic calculator, you will see the basic operators of addition, subtraction, multiplication and division. Here are the basic **mathematical operators** in Java:

+	addition (x + y)
-	subtraction (x - y)
*	multiplication (x * y)
/	division (x / y)
%	modulus – the remainder of the division of two values (x % y), e.g. 8 % 3 = 2
-	negation (-x)

There are a number of other operators in Java, called **conditional operators** and **logical operators**. They are listed below, but will be discussed further in *Chapter Four, page 39*, where we begin to look at control structures.

Conditional operators

==	is equal to
>	greater than
<	less than
>=	greater than or equal to
<=	less than or equal to
!=	not equal to

Logical operators

&&	and
!	not
||	or

Keywords

Keywords are also known as **reserved** words. These are words in a programming language that are used by the language for very specific purposes. We saw examples of their use in Chapter One. Some keywords you have used are:

```
class
```

```
public
```

```
static
```

```
void
```

```
double
```

WARNING

You should only ever use keywords for their specific purpose.

A full list of Java keywords is shown below, although it is unlikely you will use many of them:

abstract	finally	public	assert	float
return	boolean	for	short	break
static	byte	if	strictfp	case
implements	super	catch	import	switch
char	instanceof	synchronized	class	int
this	interface	throw	continue	long
throws	default	native	transient	do
new	try	double	package	void
else	private	volatile	extends	protected
while	final			

Data

As explained in Chapter One, computer programs process data. We can input data, process it, and output it. There are different types of data for us to use in Java. They fall into three main categories:

1. **Literal** data

2. **Variable** data

3. **Constant** data

Literal data is data that will never change.

We saw many examples of this in Chapter One:

```
"Please input a weight in pounds "
2.2
" kilos = "
```

All the above are examples of literal data. The literals can be numbers, such as **2.2**, or they might be strings of characters, such as " **pounds = "**.

Variable data is data that will always change.

We saw some examples of how we use variables in Chapter One:

```
s = input.next();
kilos = input.nextDouble();
pounds = kilos / 2.2;
```

All the above are examples of how we might store variable values. The first two enable the user to input variable values into the computer's memory. The third one performs a calculation by taking the variable value assigned to **kilos**, dividing it by **2.2**, and copying the result into the variable **pounds**.

> **NOTE**
>
> When we give a variable a new value, we follow the following convention to construct what we call an **assignment statement**:
>
> **variable = expression;**
>
> The expression (to the right of the equals sign) is always evaluated first. Its result is then *assigned to* the variable (to the left of the equals sign).

Variables have unique names. We invent our own names for variables. When we use variables in a Java program, we must tell the compiler what their names are, and what type of data will be stored in the variable. The naming of variables is called **variable declaration**. You saw examples of this in Chapter One:

```
String s;

double pounds, kilos;
```

The first example above declares a variable which we have called **s**. We have explicitly stated that **s** will store string data.

The second example declares two **double** variables, one called **pounds**, and one called **kilos**. Notice how they are separated by commas. A **double** variable can store fractional values, such as 3.3, -7.345, 1004.2.

String and **double** indicate the type of data that will be stored. There are many other types of data. In this book, we shall only use a small subset of these:

● **String** for text;

● **double** for fractional numbers;

● **int** for whole numbers (positive or negative);

● **boolean** for truth values (simply true or false).

We can declare as many variable values as we like in a program. Make sure every variable you declare has a meaningful use. Also make sure you declare a variable before you use it.

As stated earlier, variables must have unique names, and we invent those names.

However, there are some rules we must follow when we choose a variable name:

● A variable name must start with a letter or underscore.

● The rest of the name can be made up of letters, digits or underscores, but definitely no spaces.

● The letters can be upper or lower case, but remember that Java is case sensitive.

● You must not use a Java keyword to name a variable.

Constant data is data that may change, but not regularly.

Aa a half-way house between literals and variables, constants are useful for programs where we use values that may change in future, but only every now and again.

An example would be in a point-of-sale system, where VAT rates are used. To express a constant for this could be done like this:

```
final double rateOfVAT = 17.5;
```

A constant is used in the same way as a variable.

Exercise 2.1: Breakthrough Java

 Which of the following variable names are valid in Java?

- num
- int
- 5
- %percent
- the number

Which of the following assignment statements are valid in Java?

- average = (a + b + c + d)/3
- result = 3 x c
- six = two + five
- total tally = a + b + c + d
- share = total ÷ group
- tot = tot + 1

Write a program to input a number, add 10 to it, and output the result.

Write a program to input two numbers, multiply them together, and display the result.

EXPERT GUIDANCE

Once you complete the last two parts of the exercise above, you have achieved a major breakthrough. Not only will you have successfully built a Java program, you will have designed it too.

To be a good programmer, you need to analyse a problem, and use your creative abilities to come up with a well-designed solution, just as an architect or structural engineer would do in building a house or constructing a bridge.

The next chapter considers how you might begin to design your programs, and how you might use charting techniques to communicate your design – in other words, your program *blueprint*.

Java Forum

Post	What initial value does a variable take when I declare it? ⭐
Reply	You might think, for example, that if you declare an `int`, its initial value would be 0. Unfortunately, it isn't. No value is assigned to a variable on declaration. Many program bugs arise because the programmer forgot or omitted to **initialise** a variable. There are various ways of doing this. A good way to do it is to give your variables a value as you declare them, such as: `int i = 0;` ☺

Post	Why are there different data types? ⭐
Reply	The different data types (String, int, double, etc.) are fundamental in computer programming languages, as they dictate how data is stored and manipulated. You must be very careful to choose the most appropriate data type for your programs. For example, if you are dealing with finance, use double values for money, and if you are dealing with descriptive names, use Strings. It sounds like common sense, but it's very easy to make a mistake.

Also, be careful when writing input statements to select the correct expression for each data type. For example:

```
s = input.next(); // s is a String

pounds = input.nextDouble(); // pounds is a double

i = input.nextInt(); // i is an integer
```
☺

Post	Why is String in upper case whereas double and int are in lower case? ⭐
Reply	The reason for this will become apparent much later. Doubles and ints are known as **scalar data types**. A String is known as a **class**. They work in different ways, but for our purposes now, we don't need to explore this any further. Just make sure you use the correct case! ☺

Chapter 3

BEGINNING WITH DESIGN

Chapter overview

Any builder or engineer (whether constructing a house, a bridge, a football stadium, or an aeroplane) expects to follow a design of some description. They don't make it up as they go along. They have standards to adhere to, and their products are rigorously tested.

The same principles apply in Computing. The whole process from specification to product launch, and subsequent product maintenance, is called **Software Engineering**.

In the last chapter you were introduced to the bricks and mortar of a computer program. Now we will look at how we can use graphical techniques to help you document your design.

At the end of this chapter you will be able to:

- ✓ appreciate the fundamentals of program design;
- ✓ use a graphical technique to design simple computer programs;
- ✓ interpret program specifications and design programs to solve simple problems.

Why design is a good idea

A **program design** acts as a blueprint for the program you are about to build. The design might help to remind yourself how you constructed a program, it might help to communicate your design to others (perhaps another programmer), or it might be a method to help you use your design for a similar program in future.

> **TIP**
>
> Whatever you use your design work for, it's a good idea to get into the habit very early.

We will see that there are three types of basic building blocks (called **control structures**) for any design:

- **Sequence** – where a program steps line by line.
- **Selection** – where a program needs to make a decision.
- **Loops** – where a program needs to do the same thing a number of times.

Design notation

For each of the building blocks, we will use a specific graphical notation.

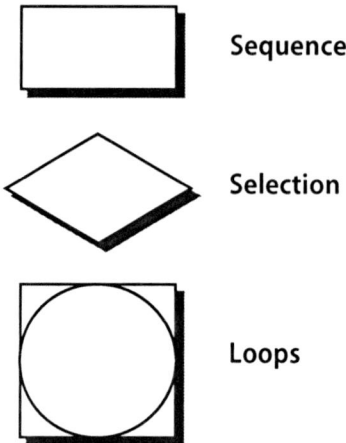

Sequence

Selection

Loops

We will use one other building block to indicate the name of the program (which is the class name near the top of your program code).

**For new
programs**

So far, we have only used the **sequence** control structure. We will deal with **selection** and **loops** later.

How to design from a specification

When we are faced with any problem, it's natural for us to break it down into smaller problems. We then solve each small problem in turn, before we achieve our ultimate goal.

For example, think about how you would solve these problems:

- make a cup of coffee;
- program a video recorder;
- describe to a stranger how to get from their hotel to the airport;
- make a paper aeroplane.

All of these are quite trivial, but it's impossible to do these without solving other problems first: fill the kettle with water, access a menu, find a bus or train timetable, fold a piece of paper in half, etc.

The same way of thinking applies for computer programming. Breaking down a program specification into smaller problems can be quite difficult, but with experience, and by following some simple guidelines, it should become much simpler.

Let's consider a program specification:

> Input the length and width of a room in metres, and calculate and display the size of carpet needed in square metres.

DESIGN GUIDELINE

Break the specification down into three *sub-problems:* Input, Process and Output.

As discussed in Chapter One, virtually all computer programs follow this three component pattern in some way, so it makes sense to start here.

Breaking our problem down yields:

- input two numbers representing the length and width of a room in metres;
- calculate the size of the carpet needed;
- display the size of the carpet needed.

Now, let's use our graphical notation to show this design:

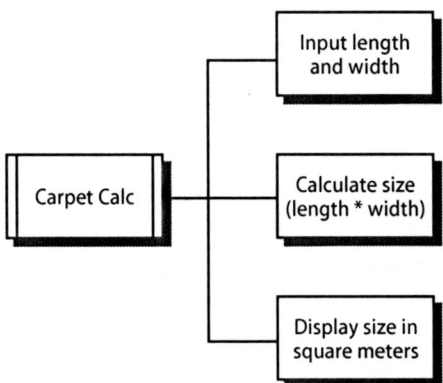

The program name is **CarpetCalc**. The sequence of events in **CarpetCalc** starts at the top of the diagram and goes down, just as your program code inevitably will.

As this is a simple program, we can now move straight on to thinking about the program code, but we still have some design decisions to make.

DESIGN GUIDELINE

Identify possible variables by looking for nouns (objects) in the program specification.

The nouns in our program specification are in bold below:

- Input the **length** and **width** of a **room** in metres, calculate and display the **size of carpet** needed in square metres.

So here are our possible variables: **length, width, size of carpet**. Let's discuss them in turn:

1. **length**: we need to input the length, and this could vary from room to room, so this looks to be a very strong candidate for a variable;

2. **width**: the same argument applies as above – a strong candidate;

3. **room**: we are only interested in the room from the point of view of its size, and we can describe that with length and width – an unlikely candidate;

4. **size of carpet**: we need to display this, and again it can vary from room to room – a strong candidate.

If we look at our design, and the candidate list above, we would be sensible to choose three variables for the program: **length, width, size of carpet**.

> **DESIGN GUIDELINE**
>
> Select the variable data types, names and initial values.

As any room is highly unlikely to be dimensioned in units of exact metres, it is common sense to use **doubles** for all variables.

Choose variable names that are self-explanatory – **length, width**, and **sizeOfCarpet** are all good ideas. Notice how **sizeOfCarpet** cleverly uses upper case for each new word to make it easier to read. This is a good habit to get into.

Sensible initial values for each of these variables would be zero, although because the user will input the **length** and **width**, and because **sizeOfCarpet** is calculated only from these variables (**sizeOfCarpet = length * width**), we don't actually need to provide initial values.

> **DESIGN GUIDELINE**
>
> Take the design chart, the variables, and the program template to construct the program.

Here is our program template:

```java
import java.util.Scanner;

/* This program … */
class ???
{
    public static void main(String[] args)
    {
        Scanner input = new Scanner(System.in);
    }
}
```

Change the class name and the program comment to:

```
import java.util.Scanner;

/* Input the length and width of a room in metres, calculate
and display the size of carpet needed in square metres */
class CarpetCalc
{
   public static void main(String[] args)
   {
       Scanner input = new Scanner(System.in);
   }
}
```

 Taking the wording from the boxes in our design, we can add some more comments to the program:

```
import java.util.Scanner;

/* Input the length and width of a room in metres, calculate
and display the size of carpet needed in square metres */
class CarpetCalc
{
   public static void main(String[] args)
   {
       Scanner input = new Scanner(System.in);

       // input length and width

       // calculate size

       // display size
   }
}
```

What we have done above is add some new **program comments**. We can write program comments **ANYWHERE** in a program.

EXPERT GUIDANCE

There are two ways of writing program comments. The first way is best for long comments which cover several lines:

```
/* Input the length and width of a room in metres,
calculate and display the size of carpet needed in square
metres */
```

The second way is best for short, snappy comments:

```
// input length and width
```

The next step is to add the variable declarations to the program. Note how they are declared immediately after the line which begins: **Scanner input = ...;**

```java
import java.util.Scanner;

/* Input the length and width of a room in metres, calculate
and display the size of carpet needed in square metres */
class CarpetCalc
{
    public static void main(String[] args)
    {
        Scanner input = new Scanner(System.in);

        double length, width, sizeOfCarpet;

        // input length and width

        // calculate size

        // display size
    }
}
```

 Now we can add the rest of the code.

This is the most difficult part and may take several tries, so don't worry if it doesn't work first time!

```
import java.util.Scanner;

/* Input the length and width of a room in metres, calculate
and display the size of carpet needed in square metres */
class CarpetCalc
{
    public static void main(String[] args)
    {
        Scanner input = new Scanner(System.in);

        double length, width, sizeOfCarpet;

        // input length and width
        System.out.print("Please input the length of the room
        ");
        length = input.nextDouble();
        System.out.print("Please input the width of the room
        ");
        width = input.nextDouble();

        // calculate size
        sizeOfCarpet = length * width;

        // display size
        System.out.print("Carpet needed = " + sizeOfCarpet +
        " sq.m");
    }
}
```

▶ Save the program as **CarpetCalc.java**.

▶ Finally, compile and run the program.

```
C:\WINDOWS\system32\cmd.exe

C:\Java>javac CarpetCalc.java

C:\Java>java CarpetCalc
Please input the length of the room 10
Please input the width of the room 5
Carpet needed = 50.0 sq.m
C:\Java>_
```

Exercise 3.1: Carpet cost

 Assuming the carpet for the room described in the worked example costs £5.00 per square metre, amend the program to calculate and display the cost of the required amount of carpet.

Exercise 3.2: Age in 2050

 Design and build a program to input the year in which you were born and display the age you will be in the year 2050.

Exercise 3.3: Average

 Design and build a program to input a set of 4 numbers and display their average (be careful with data types!)

Exercise 3.4: Money

 Design and build a program to input the number of £5, £10 and £20 notes you have, then display the total number of notes and the total amount of money.

The next chapter will introduce the second of the three control structures: **Selection**.

Java Forum

Post	What makes a good program? ★
Reply	A program should be well-designed, easy to read, well laid out, and of course, it should work!

A program should be well-designed, easy to read, well laid out, and of course, it should work!

There are many ways to write the same program. In fact, it is highly unlikely that two people will produce exactly the same solution independently.

Consider an alternative solution to the **CarpetCalc** program:

```java
import java.util.Scanner;

/* Input the length and width of a room in metres,
calculate and display the size of carpet needed in
square metres */
class CarpetCalc
{
    public static void main(String[] args)
    {
        Scanner input = new Scanner(System.in);

        double l, w;

        // input length and width
        System.out.print("Length? ");
        l = input.nextDouble();
        System.out.print("Width? ");
        w = input.nextDouble();

        // calculate and display size
        System.out.print("Carpet needed = " + (l*w) + "
        sq.m");
    }
}
```

The new program differs from our original solution in two main ways:

1. It looks a little 'lazy'. The programmer has used variable names that aren't self-explanatory, and the user prompts (messages to the user) are crude.

2. Only two variables are used, as the calculation of the carpet size is done in the display statement.

☺

EXPERT GUIDANCE

Whatever you think of the above observations, the program still works. It conforms to the original design, but one might argue that it is not so well **engineered** as the original solution.

Chapter 4

SELECTION

Chapter overview

By now we should know that Java programs execute in sequence, line by line. We should also know that programs help us solve problems. When we express a problem solution, we can express it in sub-problems, to make it easier to solve. However, not all sub-problems and their solutions apply in all cases. In this chapter, we will look at programs where decisions need to be made, depending on some external event such as a user's input selection.

At the end of this chapter you will be able to:

- ✓ design programs that use selections (decisions);
- ✓ write Java programs using the appropriate Java rules;
- ✓ use some fairly complex logic to solve problems and apply those solutions in Java;
- ✓ write programs that validate a user's input.

Decisions, decisions!

Consider the following simple real-world problem:

Depending on the weather, should I wear my sunglasses or take out a coat?

In this problem, we need to **select** from two options:

- either wear sunglasses; or
- take out a coat.

Most computer programs need to make such selections. For example:

- a one or two player computer game?
- a receipt or no receipt for a cash machine transaction?

As you can see from the question marks, selections usually go hand in hand with questions.

Let's consider how we might re-word our weather problem, to move towards how we might express it in a computer language:

```
What's the weather like?
```

```
If the weather is good wear sunglasses
```

```
Else take out a coat
```

In Java, the code for a program to advise us on what to do would look similar in structure to what we see above. However, of course, we need to use the proper language rules (or **syntax**) for our solution:

```
// what's the weather like?
```

```
System.out.print("Is the weather good today (y/n)? ");
```

```
goodWeather = input.next();
```

Above, we have a **String** called **goodWeather**, which will store **y** or **n**, depending on what the user has typed.

The next thing we need to do is check the value of weather, and advise the user accordingly:

```
if (goodWeather.equals("y"))
    System.out.print("Wear sunglasses!");
else
    System.out.print("Take out a coat!");
```

Putting this all together in a program may give us:

```java
import java.util.Scanner;

/* Ask the user about the weather, advise them to wear
shades or take out a coat */
class WeatherAdvisor
{
   public static void main(String[] args)
   {
      Scanner input = new Scanner(System.in);

      String goodWeather;

      // what's the weather like?
      System.out.print("Is the weather good today (y/n)? ");
      goodWeather = input.next();

      if (goodWeather.equals("y"))
          System.out.print("Wear sunglasses!");
      else
          System.out.print("Take out a coat!");
   }
}
```

```
C:\WINDOWS\system32\cmd.exe

C:\Java>java WeatherAdvisor
Is the weather good today (y/n)? n
Take out a coat!
C:\Java>java WeatherAdvisor
Is the weather good today (y/n)? y
Wear sunglasses!
C:\Java>
```

Let's now take a closer look at the selection we have just made, bit by bit. We will introduce some new terminology too.

The code that asks the user about the weather looks like this:

```java
// what's the weather like?
```

```java
System.out.print("Is the weather good today (y/n)? ");
```

```java
goodWeather = input.next();
```

The first line is simply a program comment.

The next line asks the question **Is the weather good today (y/n)?**

The last line enables the user to type in their answer, **y** or **n**.

Next, we introduce two new **keywords: if** and **else**. These words mean exactly the same as they do in English.

Immediately after the **if**, comes a **test condition**. In Java, a test condition is **ALWAYS** enclosed in round brackets, and it **ALWAYS** evaluates to either **true**, or **false**. So basically, we have here a test which either passes (it's true), or fails (it's false).

In our example, the test condition is:

`(goodWeather.equals("y")).`

We might read this as:

is goodWeather equal to y?

NOTE

Notice there is NO SEMI-COLON at the end of the line.

You should **never** use a semi-colon in an **if** or **else** clause.

WARNING

A variable name must start with a letter or underscore.

The rest of the name can be made up of letters, digits or underscores, but definitely no spaces.

The letters can be upper or lower case, but remember that Java is case sensitive.

You must not use a Java keyword to name a variable.

Let's consider the next line:

`System.out.print("Wear sunglasses!");`

This line appears immediately after the test condition. It runs only when the test condition is true, in our case only when **goodWeather** is equal to **y**. Under any other circumstance, this line is ignored when the program runs.

The next line contains a solitary **else**. Notice how the **else** does not have a test condition associated with it. Only the **if** has a test condition. Also notice that the **else** doesn't have a semi-colon, just like the **if**.

After the **else** comes the final line of the overall condition:

`System.out.print("Take out a coat!");`

By now, you've probably realised that this statement only executes when the test fails, in our example that is where **goodWeather** is anything other than **y**.

Designing selections

In the previous chapter, we talked about program design. You were introduced to the design notation for **sequence**, **selection**, and **loops**. As a reminder, here is the symbol for a selection:

We will now use this notation to demonstrate how to use selection in design. The design for our weather program looks like this:

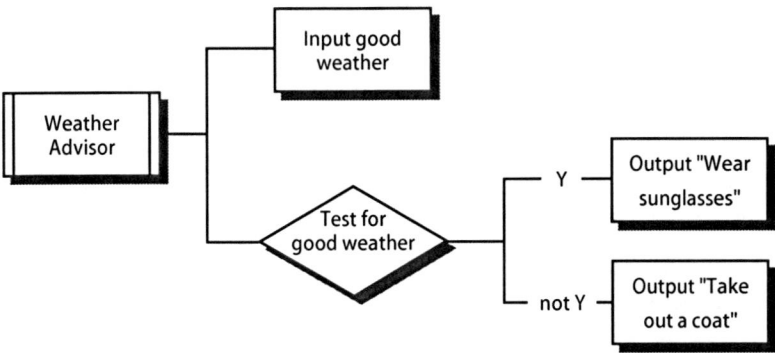

Remember how the sequence of a program design flows from top to bottom. However, the selection causes a change of direction from left to right. The idea here is that you can read the program design more easily by looking at it in varying levels of detail.

Starting with the left-most box, we can see that the program is a weather advisor.

Moving in (or indenting) to the next column of boxes, we can see that the program comprises an input, followed by a test. The next column shows us what the results of the test should do.

DESIGN GUIDELINE

Stepwise refinement

There is another important reason why the design is presented in this left-to-right fashion. Remember how we looked at solving larger problems by breaking them down into smaller **sub-problems**? In program design, we often call this process **stepwise refinement**. This simply means that we refine a design step by step, in increasing levels of detail, until we are confident that we can use the design to write a program.

In our weather program, we needn't worry about *what we do* about good weather, until we have solved the problem of asking the user for the information. So firstly, we might solve the *higher-level* problem of getting the information, before we actually decide what to do with it, like this:

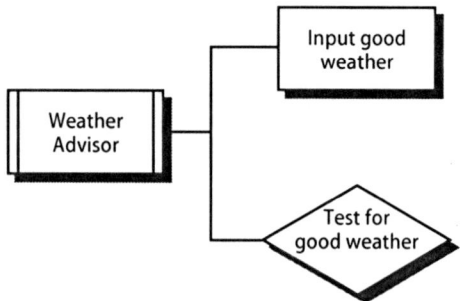

So the basic structure of the design involves:

- input good weather;

- test for good weather.

Once we are happy with that structure, we might then go on to **detail** what the test does, by adding the other boxes:

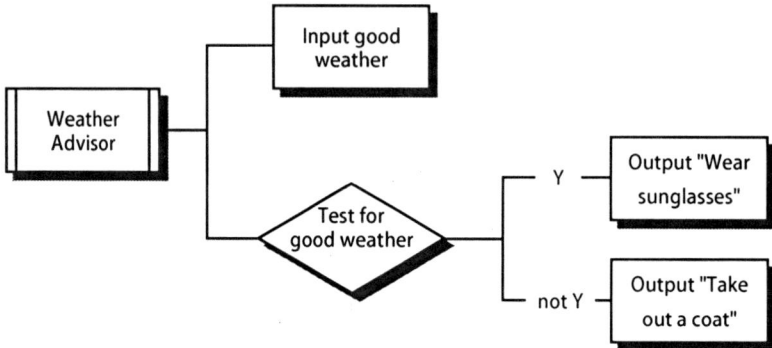

DESIGN GUIDELINE

Indent your code

This design guideline refers to the **layout design** of your code. You may have noticed in our weather program how the code *inside* the `if` ... `else` construct is indented a few spaces:

```
if (goodWeather.equals("y"))
    System.out.print("Wear sunglasses!");
else
    System.out.print("Take out a coat!");
```

The principle here is that the code is simpler to read if it is indented in this way. It's very easy to see where the `if` ends and where the else starts. Notice how this indentation also reflects how the boxes in the design diagram are laid out too.

When your programs get more complex, you will realise that good indentation can be crucial.

Only when we can see that no more detail needs to be added, should we take our design and use it to program the solution.

Exercise 4.1: Capital city

 Design, write and test a program which asks the user to input the capital city of France.

 If they answer **Paris**, give them a congratulations message.

More on selection

We have so far seen a simple application of selection. We will now introduce some more complex issues.

What if we want to do more than one thing in a selection? Our weather program only outputs a simple message for each weather case. Suppose we want to add some more messages: in good weather, let's advise our user not to forget sun screen, and in bad weather, we'll tell them not to forget their brolly.

Modifying our original design would give us:

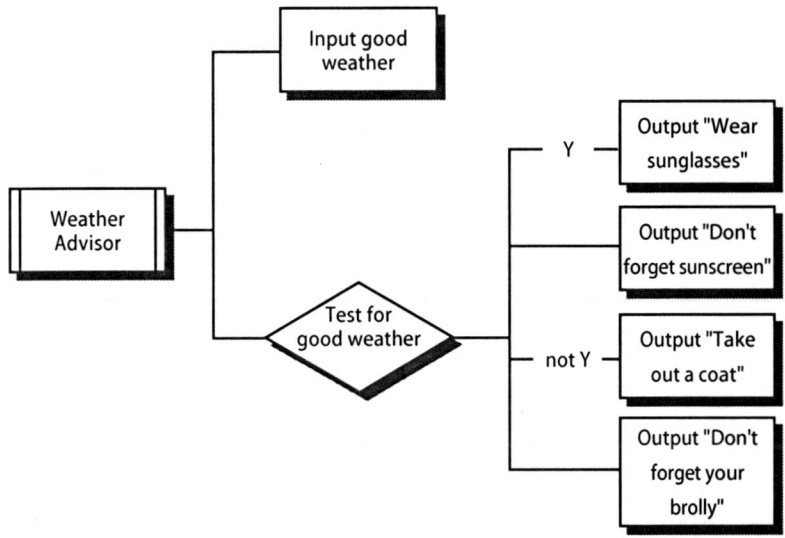

Notice how we have added two new boxes. When good weather is equal to **y**, we now do two things, and when it's *not y*, we also do two things.

The program code for this modification looks like this:

```
if (goodWeather.equals("y"))
{
    System.out.println("Wear sunglasses!");
    System.out.print("Don't forget sunscreen!");
}
else
{
    System.out.println("Take out a coat!");
    System.out.print("Don't forget your brolly!");
}
```

Notice how we use the word **println** instead of **print**. The difference between these is that **print** does not place the cursor on a new line after that line runs, whereas **println** does (**println** can be read as **print line** to remind you in future what it means).

It's important to note that as well as adding the new messages, we have had to add some curly brackets. These curly brackets indicate the range of statements we want to execute when the test is true, and where it is false. Our first post in *Chapter One, page 21*, told us what curly brackets mean. The answer was: they mean **Begin** and **End**. In the example above, you might read the curly brackets as: **Begin if, End if, Begin else, End else**.

Putting the whole program together gives us:

```java
import java.util.Scanner;

/* Ask the user about the weather, advise them to wear
shades and take sunscreen or take out a coat and brolly */
class WeatherAdvisor
{
   public static void main(String[] args)
   {
      Scanner input = new Scanner(System.in);

      String goodWeather;

      // what's the weather like?
      System.out.print("Is the weather good today (y/n)?
      ");
      goodWeather = input.next();

      if (goodWeather.equals("y"))
      {
          System.out.println("Wear sunglasses!");
          System.out.print("Don't forget sunscreen!");
      }
      else
      {
          System.out.println("Take out a coat!");
          System.out.print("Don't forget your brolly!");
      }

   }
}
```

EXPERT GUIDANCE

One thing to note about this program is the number of curly brackets. You can see that each open curly bracket has a corresponding close curly bracket. You should also be able to see easily which ones match to which, simply by scanning from the top to the bottom of the program. Hopefully, you should now appreciate the power of **indentation**.

In case you are not convinced, the same program with no indentation is shown on the next page.

```
import java.util.Scanner;

/* Ask the user about the weather, and advise them to wear
shades and take sunscreen or take out a coat and brolly */
class WeatherAdvisor
{
public static void main(String[] args)
{
Scanner input = new Scanner(System.in);

String goodWeather;

// what's the weather like?
System.out.print("Is the weather good today (y/n)? ");
goodWeather = input.next();

if (goodWeather.equals("y"))
{
System.out.println("Wear sunglasses!");
System.out.print("Don't forget sunscreen!");
}
else
{
System.out.println("Take out a coat!");
System.out.print("Don't forget your brolly!");
}
}
}
```

Not so clear now is it!

NOTE

In fact, there is an intentional error in this program. Can you spot it?
The error would be clearer to see if we used appropriate indentation.

Here is the code again and you can easily see that there is a closing curly bracket missing.

```java
import java.util.Scanner;

/* Ask the user about the weather, and advise them to wear
shades and take sunscreen or take out a coat and brolly */
class WeatherAdvisor
{
   public static void main(String[] args)
   {
       Scanner input = new Scanner(System.in);

       String goodWeather;

       // what's the weather like?
       System.out.print("Is the weather good today (y/n)?
       ");
       goodWeather = input.next();

       if (goodWeather.equals("y"))
       {
           System.out.println("Wear sunglasses!");
           System.out.print("Don't forget sunscreen!");
       }
       else
       {
           System.out.println("Take out a coat!");
           System.out.print("Don't forget your brolly!");


   }
}
```

Missing closing curly
bracket should be here.

EXPERT GUIDANCE

Remember, every open curly bracket has a corresponding close, and if you use indentation, you should be able to see easily which ones match to which, simply by scanning from the top to the bottom of the program.

The conditional operators

In *Chapter Two, page 23*, we discussed the *bricks and mortar* of a Java program. We introduced operators, including conditional operators. They are used when we are comparing **numerical** values with one another. Here they are again:

==	is equal to (note that this is two equals signs placed together – often called **double equals**)
>	greater than
<	less than
>=	greater than or equal to
<=	less than or equal to
!=	not equal to

So far, we have only compared strings with one another. We can use the conditional operators in a similar way.

Here are some examples:

```
// old enough to drink?
if (age >= 18)
    System.out.println("Have a glass of wine!");
else
    System.out.println("Have a glass of cola!");


// can you draw a state pension?
if (age < 65)
    statePension = 0;
else
    statePension = 100;


// 10 out of 10?
if (score == 10)
    System.out.println("Congratulations!");


// discount the bill by 10% if it's over £100
if (bill > 100)
{
        discount = bill * 0.1;
        bill = bill - discount;

}
```

Exercise 4.2: Income and expenditure

 Design, write and test a program which asks the user their income and expenditure, and output "SPEND SPEND SPEND!", or "Put some money in the bank!" depending on the outcome.

Exercise 4.3: Meal cost

 Design, write and test a program which asks a waiter the cost of a customer's meal.

 If the cost is £10 or more, give a 5% discount.

The logical operators

Logical operators were introduced in *Chapter Two, page 24.* They are used for complex conditions where we need to know the results of *more than one test* before doing something.

There are three logical operators:

&&   and

!   not

|| or

As an example of how we use logical operators, suppose we wanted to be more specific about the weather in our weather program. Let's say we will only wear sunglasses and take sun screen if the weather is good AND the sky is clear. We would need two variables for this, and we would need to test for both of them before passing the test condition.

This is how our code might look:

```
String goodWeather, clear;

// what's the weather like?
System.out.print("Is the weather good today (y/n)? ");
goodWeather = input.next();
// is it cloudless?
System.out.print("Is the sky clear (y/n)? ");
clear = input.next();

if (goodWeather.equals("y") && clear.equals("y"))
{
    System.out.println("Wear sunglasses!");
    System.out.print("Don't forget sunscreen!");
}
else
{
    System.out.println("Take out a coat!");
    System.out.print("Don't forget your brolly!");
}
```

This is the new test condition:

```
if (goodWeather.equals("y") && clear.equals("y"))
```

Notice that we now have two tests in the test condition (inside the round brackets). The two tests stand independently.

> **WARNING**
>
> A common mistake in Java is to combine wrongly separate tests. Here are a couple of examples:
>
> ```
> // don't do it like this!!
> if (goodWeather && clear.equals("y"))
>
> // and don't do it like this!!
> if (clear.equals("y" || "Y"))
> ```
>
> In the above example, the programmer has attempted to cover for the user typing an upper case *Y* or a lower case *y*. It is of course good practice to program for this possibility. The correct way to do this is to separate the tests out:
>
> ```
> // this is the way to do it!!
> if (clear.equals("y") || clear.equals("Y"))
> ```

Here's a very complex condition, which covers the new requirement for the weather program, as well as taking into account upper or lower case input:

```
if ( (goodWeather.equals("y") || goodWeather.equals("Y")) &&
     (clear.equals("y") || clear.equals("Y")) )
```

Notice how round brackets are used to separate out the tests. The tests inside the innermost brackets are always evaluated first. The condition spans two lines on the page, but that has been done purely for neatness and program readability. It doesn't actually matter how many lines you use for a condition (or any other line in Java). Now our programs are becoming more complex, program statements may well span more than one line.

Data validation

A powerful use of selection constructs such as **if** ... **else** is where we want to check the validity of data.

To illustrate data validation, let's consider an example:

> **Design, write and test a program which asks the user to input a number between one and six.**
>
> **As long as the user has input a number *in range*, output the square and cube of that number. Otherwise, inform the user that the number is *out of range*.**

Here's a solution to the problem, starting with the design, then the code:

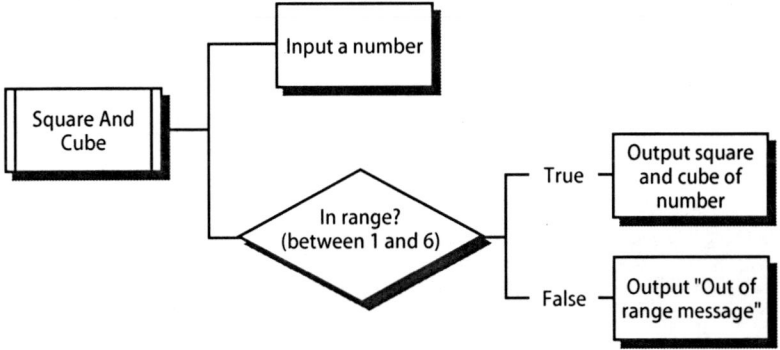

```
import java.util.Scanner;

/* Ask the user to input a number between 1 and 6. Output
   the square and cube of the number, as long as it's in
   range */
class SquareAndCube
{
    public static void main(String[] args)
    {
        Scanner input = new Scanner(System.in);

        int aNumber;

        System.out.print("Please input a number between 1 and
        6 ");
        aNumber = input.nextInt();

        if ( aNumber >= 1 && aNumber <= 6 )
        {
            System.out.println("The square of " + aNumber +
                " is: " + (aNumber*aNumber) );
            System.out.println("The cube of " + aNumber +
                " is: " + (aNumber*aNumber*aNumber) );
        }
        else
            System.out.println("The number is out of
            range!");

    }
}
```

So, by carefully using combinations of conditional and logical operators, we can **filter** our data, and perform different actions depending on their values.

Sometimes, selection in computer programs can be very confusing. To illustrate how complex things can get, consider the following example in Java (it uses all the conditional and logical operators):

```
if ( ( aNumber >= 1 && aNumber <= 10 && aNumber != 4  ) ||
     ( aNumber < 20 && aNumber > 14 && !(aNumber == 18) )
```

Translated into English, this means:

If **aNumber** is greater than or equal to 1 and less than or equal to 10, but not equal to 4 OR it's less than 20 and greater than 14, but not 18, then the test passes.

In other words, the numbers 1, 2, 3, 5, 6, 7, 8, 9, 10, 15, 16, 17 and 19 are all valid numbers for the test.

> **WARNING**
>
> A very common mistake in programming happens where a programmer knows in his or her own mind exactly what they want to do in the program, but find difficulty in translating that into the programming language.

It's a good idea to get into the habit of using the type of logic we use in computer programs. Here is an exercise to help you get started:

Exercise 4.4: Logic teaser

Below is a table. Columns 1 and 2 indicate two tests, A and B. As we know, tests always evaluate to true (T) and false (F). The rows of the table indicate combinations of the possible values for A and B. The other columns in the table show more complex tests which use A and B in various combinations along with conditional and logical operators.

 Fill out the rest of the table for each row, given the True/False values of A and B. To start you off, the first complex condition (A or B) has been completed.

A	B	A||B	A&&B	!(A||B)	!(A&&B)	!A||B	!(!A&&!B)	A||!B
T	T	T						
T	F	T						
F	T	T						
F	F	F						

Nested selection

So far, we have seen the `if` … `else` construct used in varying forms of complexity. That complexity has so far been determined by the test condition (the bit in the round brackets after the `if`).

Now we will introduce other ways of dealing with complexity in selection.

Consider the following example:

> Design, write and test a program which asks a user to input their age. If they are at least 18, we can then ask them if they would like a glass of wine (W) or a pint of beer (B), which they should be charged for at £3.00 or £2.50 respectively.

There are many ways to write a program to solve this problem. The first thing to do, of course, is to analyse the program specification.

So far, two of our design guidelines advise us to break the specification down into three **sub-problems: input**, **process** and **output**, and to use stepwise refinement to develop our solution.

Putting these into practice for our example might give us the following first-cut design:

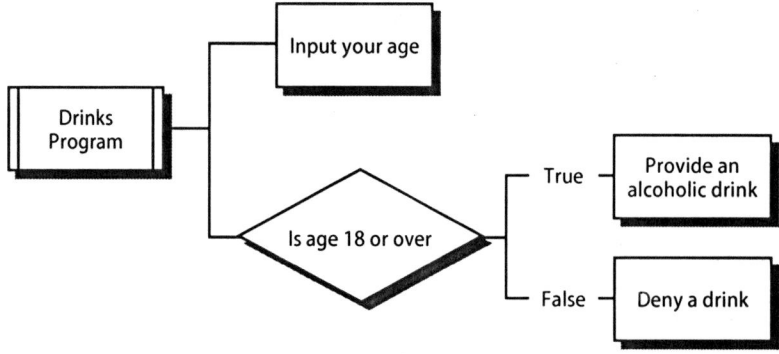

EXPERT GUIDANCE

You may notice that this design structure is very similar to a number of others we have already seen and used. It's worth noting that many computer programs follow *patterns*, and that with experience, you will be able to *re-use* such *patterns* in different combinations to solve many problems.

The design above is useful for us to see how our program might be structured, but we need to add to the design to show how we would deal with the additional requirement of asking the user if they would like a glass of wine or beer. Let's isolate and solve that very **sub-problem**.

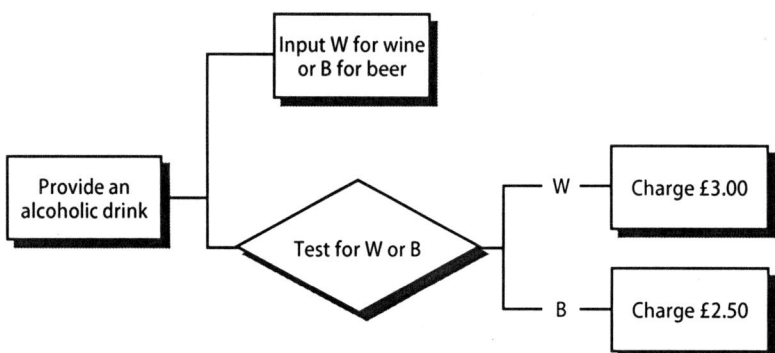

Again, our pattern is the same. Put simply, this pattern inputs something, tests it, and deals with two possible outcomes.

Now all we need to do is incorporate the two structures into one:

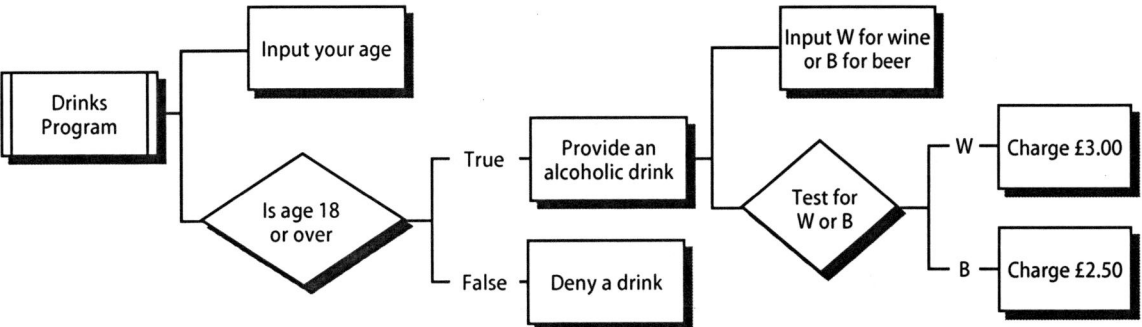

In the complete design above, we can see two selections:

● *age is 18 or over*; and

● *test for W or B.*

The second of these is nested *inside* the first. This is what we call a **nested selection**.

Let's see what this might look like in Java:

```java
import java.util.Scanner;

/* Drinks program. Offer wine of beer as long as the user is
   old enough */
class Drinks
{
    public static void main(String[] args)
    {
        Scanner input = new Scanner(System.in);

        int age;
        String drink;

        System.out.print("Please input your age ");
        age = input.nextInt();

        if (age >= 18)
        {
            System.out.print
            ("Would you like a wine (W) or beer (B)? ");
            drink = input.next();

            if (drink.equals("W"))
                    System.out.print("That will be £3.00");
            else
                    System.out.print("That will be £2.50");

        }
        else
            System.out.print("Come back when you are old
            enough!");

    }
}
```

> **NOTE**
>
> Nested selection is a very powerful technique in programming. The example on the previous page uses a single level of nested selection. More complex programs can have many levels, `ifs` inside `ifs` inside `ifs`, etc.

Multiple selection

Let's consider the drinks program in a little more detail. Specifically, let's look at the part of the program that processes our drink selection:

```
if (drink.equals("W"))

    System.out.print("That will be £3.00");

else

    System.out.print("That will be £2.50");
```

In English, this code says:

if the drink is W (i.e. wine), charge the user £3.00, otherwise charge the user £2.50.

This may be OK if we assume that the user will always type in W or B, as typing B would fail the test, and the user would be charged £2.50, which is the correct amount.

However, what if the user typed something else, such as Q? The program would charge the user for a beer, which may not have been what was intended – perhaps the user aimed for W on the keyboard, and accidentally hit Q instead.

What we have here is a **data validation** problem.

We have discussed data validation already, and have seen how we might filter our data according to our requirements. There are a number of ways we could solve our drinks problem here. Using what we know already, we might produce something like this:

```
if ( drink.equals("W") || drink.equals("B") )
{
    if (drink.equals("W"))
        System.out.print("That will be £3.00");
    else
        System.out.print("That will be £2.50");
}
else
    System.out.print("Sorry, that is not an option!");
```

Here, we have used a new **if** … **else** construct to *trap* a possible input error. This works fine, but perhaps a better way would be to use a new construct, which we call an *else if*.

Here's how we might use it in our program:

```
if (drink.equals("W"))
    System.out.print("That will be £3.00");
else if (drink.equals("B"))
    System.out.print("That will be £2.50");
```

Instead of using simply an **else** in our program, we can combine **else** with a new **if** to perform a stronger form of testing. The syntax for the **if** part of the **else if** is just the same as in our previous uses of the **if** clause.

We can still use the **else** on its own in combination with **if** and **else if**. Note however, that it always comes last in the overall condition:

```
if (drink.equals("W"))
    System.out.print("That will be £3.00");
else if (drink.equals("B"))
    System.out.print("That will be £2.50");
else
    System.out.print("Sorry, that is not an option!");
```

We can use many **else if** clauses in combination to form larger tests. Let's assume that our drinks program has a new requirement to cover some new drinks – cider (C) at £2.00, and vodka (V) at £1.50:

```
if (drink.equals("W"))
    System.out.print("That will be £3.00");
else if (drink.equals("B"))
    System.out.print("That will be £2.50");
else if (drink.equals("C"))
    System.out.print("That will be £2.00");
else if (drink.equals("V"))
    System.out.print("That will be £1.50");
else
    System.out.print("Sorry, that is not an option!");
```

And now, another requirement, that there are two types of beer – lager (L) at £2.75 and ale (A) at £2.50:

```
if (drink.equals("W"))
    System.out.print("That will be £3.00");
else if (drink.equals("B"))
{
    System.out.print("Lager (L) or Ale (A) ? ");
    drink = input.next();
```

```
    if (drink.equals("L"))
        System.out.print("That will be £2.75");
    else if (drink.equals("A"))
        System.out.print("That will be £2.50");
    else System.out.print("Sorry, that is not an option!");
}
else if (drink.equals("C"))
    System.out.print("That will be £2.00");
else if (drink.equals("V"))
    System.out.print("That will be £1.50");
else
    System.out.print("Sorry, that is not an option!");
```

Exercise 4.5: Payday

 Design, code and test a program which inputs a code for the name of a day ("Sun" for Sunday, "Wk" for other Day) together with 2 numbers representing normal hours worked and overtime hours worked.

 Output the day name and the pay according to the following rules:

Sunday: ordinary hours @ £15 per hour; overtime @ £20 per hour .

Other day: ordinary hours @ £8 per hour; overtime @ £12.00 per hour.

Exercise 4.6: Insurance

Bike Direct insurance offers bike insurance as follows:

> basic rate = £30
> add £10 for a mountain bike
> add £5 for cyclists under 25.

 Design, write and test a program to input the type of bike – mountain or touring, and the cyclist's age, and calculate and display the premium payable.

That ends the chapter on selection. We have covered many new topics, and introduced many new programming techniques. Don't worry at this stage if you haven't understood all of them, or feel comfortable using the many different forms of selection. In the following chapters, we will be using selection more to help you become familiar with all the concepts presented here.

Java Forum

Post	It doesn't work – why not!!! ★

Reply

Here are some common selection mistakes that programmers make:

```
if x == 1    // forgot the brackets!!
if {x == 1} // it's the wrong brackets!!
if (x = 1)   /* the most common one - use DOUBLE
                EQUALS!! */
if (x => 1) /* don't you mean >= read as 'greater than
                or equals'? */
if (x =< 1) /* don't you mean <= read as 'less than or
                equals'? */

if (x == 1)
    ...
else (x == 2) // this won't work - should be else if!!
    ...

// and finally
if (x == 1);  /* don't put a semi-colon at the end of
                this line!!!! */
    ...
else;         // or this one!!!!
    ...
```
☺

Post	My selection doesn't work properly and I don't understand why! ★

Reply

Mistakes occur when programmers wrongly construct their selections. Here is a very common one, where a test is true if a variable is one of two things (such as testing a response for upper and lower case values). For example:

```
if (!answer.equals("N") || !answer.equals("n"))
```

The above selection might be read as:

if the answer isn't N or n, then the test is true.

However, this is not the case. What actually is happening here is:

if the answer isn't N or alternatively isn't n, then the test is true.

In fact, this test will ALWAYS evaluate to *true*, as the answer is ALWAYS going to be either not *N* or not *n* – it can't be two things at once!
☺

The correct logic for this would be:

```
if (!answer.equals("N") && !answer.equals("n")) /* use
AND not OR!!! */
```

As a postscript to this, consider an interesting comparison:

```
if (answer.equals("Y") || answer.equals("y"))
```

The above condition might be an alternative way of programming the test. That is, testing for a positive response (in this case *Y* or *y*), instead of the negative (*N* or *n*). In fact, in logic the two tests give the same result – *a or b* is the same as *not a and not b*! Note also that *not(a and b)* is also the same – look at your answers in the logic table exercise!

Post	**I want to compare words and sentences. How do I do that?**
Reply	The answer to this is that it's just the same as testing single character strings. Below is a small program which shows how to compare a string of words with another in Java.

```java
import java.util.Scanner;

/* a guessing game */
class GuessMyName
{
    public static void main (String [] args)
    {
        Scanner input = new Scanner(System.in);

        String teddy;

        System.out.println("Guess the teddy bear's name
        and win him! ");

        teddy = input.nextLine(); /* a full line of
        text, including spaces */

        if ( teddy.equalsIgnoreCase("Winnie The Pooh") )
            System.out.println ("That's my name! Take me
            with you!");
        else
            System.out.println ("Never heard of him!");
    }

}
```

We could have used **teddy.equals** for this program if we wanted, but this example introduces a neat way of comparing the strings without being worried about the case of the text by using **teddy.equalsIgnoreCase** instead. Note that we could have used this technique in the previous posts, when we were using more complex conditions to test for both upper and lower case, e.g

```
if (answer.equalsIgnoreCase("Y"))
```

is the same as:

```
if (answer.equals("Y") || answer.equals("y"))
```

By now you've probably realised that there is a lot more to selection than you might have first thought. It can be very complicated. Perhaps the most important thing you should do when you build any kind of complexity into your programs is to make sure you test them thoroughly, which leads us nicely onto the next post. ☺

Post | **What makes a thorough test?**

This is a difficult question. Good program testing comes with experience, when you've been around the block a few times and have experienced the typical kinds of pitfalls that programmers and program designers stumble into. However, there are ways of approaching your testing in a methodical way, and if you follow a good plan, you can maximise the chances of your program working properly in all cases.

There are tried-and-tested methods for program testing, and we will introduce some of the principles as we go along. As this chapter is all about selection, here are a couple of important things to consider when testing your conditions:

1. Test for all cases

Make sure you test for all possible ways through a condition. If you have an **if** ... **else**, that makes two, if you have an **if** ... **else if** ... **else**, that makes three, and so on.

2. Test for just either side of any boundary conditions

A *boundary condition* is one that uses one of the following conditions: **>**, **>=**, **<**, **<=**. If you use one of these conditions, you are testing for a **range** of values. For example, you might be testing for the age range for a pensioner, or the date range for a holiday, or the cost range for a particular discount. For these types of test, be careful to test for *each side* of the condition, as close to the boundary as possible.

As an illustration, let's consider the bike insurance program, from the exercises in this chapter. In that program, you probably have a condition similar to this:

```
if (age < 25)
    premium = premium + 5;
```

For this condition, you should of course make sure you test for an age of greater than 25, and less than 25 to make sure your program produces the right answer. However, if you chose the test values of say, 30 and 12, how can you be sure your program is correct? Using such arbitrary values would result in the correct premium if the following conditions were used in place of the correct one above:

```
if (age < 28)
    premium = premium + 5;
if (age <= 25)
    premium = premium + 5;
```

Whilst you might think that the first wrong example here is just plain stupid, the second one is a little more subtle, and it's a common mistake that many programmers make. They use the wrong **conditional operator** for the test. In this case, the programmer has used **<=** instead of **<**. The test would work for all conditions except for where the age is actually equal to 25. A 25 year old would wrongly be charged £5 extra for the bike insurance. If you look at the wording in the exercise, it clearly states that only people aged *under* 25 should be charged an extra fiver.

The moral of this story is that when you test your programs, make sure you test as close to either side of the boundary as you can. In our example, it would be a wise move to test for ages of 24 and 25. You should then be confident that it will work for other values. Having said that, it would do no harm to test for other, more arbitrary values too.

Chapter 5

LOOPS

Chapter overview

So far, we have experienced sequence and selection in our programs.

We will now introduce the third, and final basic control structure in computer programming: **loops** – where a program needs to do the same thing a number of times.

At the end of this chapter you will be able to:

- ✓ design and write Java programs that perform repetitive tasks;
- ✓ use a technique called the *dry run* to test your program and design logic;
- ✓ select the right kind of loop construct for a given task;
- ✓ appreciate the need for programs that contain more than one method.

Introducing loops

To illustrate the use of loops, let's consider a simple problem, where we want to separate red and black cards in a standard pack:

Take a pack of cards, and turn over each card. If it's red, place it in the *reds pile*, and if it's black, place it in the *blacks pile*.

Let's design a solution to this problem, firstly for one card:

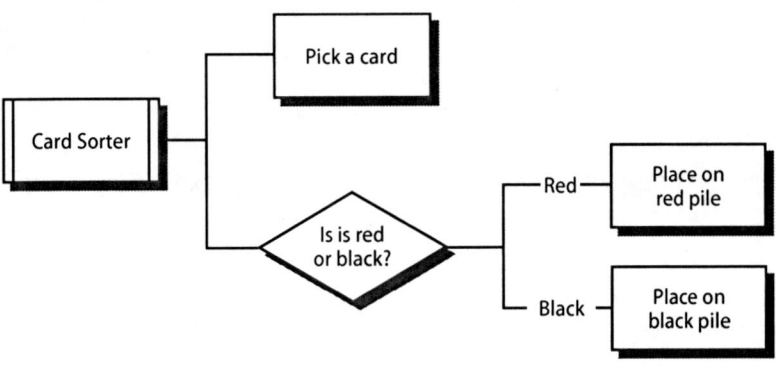

We do the same thing for the next card, and the next one, and so on. For three cards, we might have:

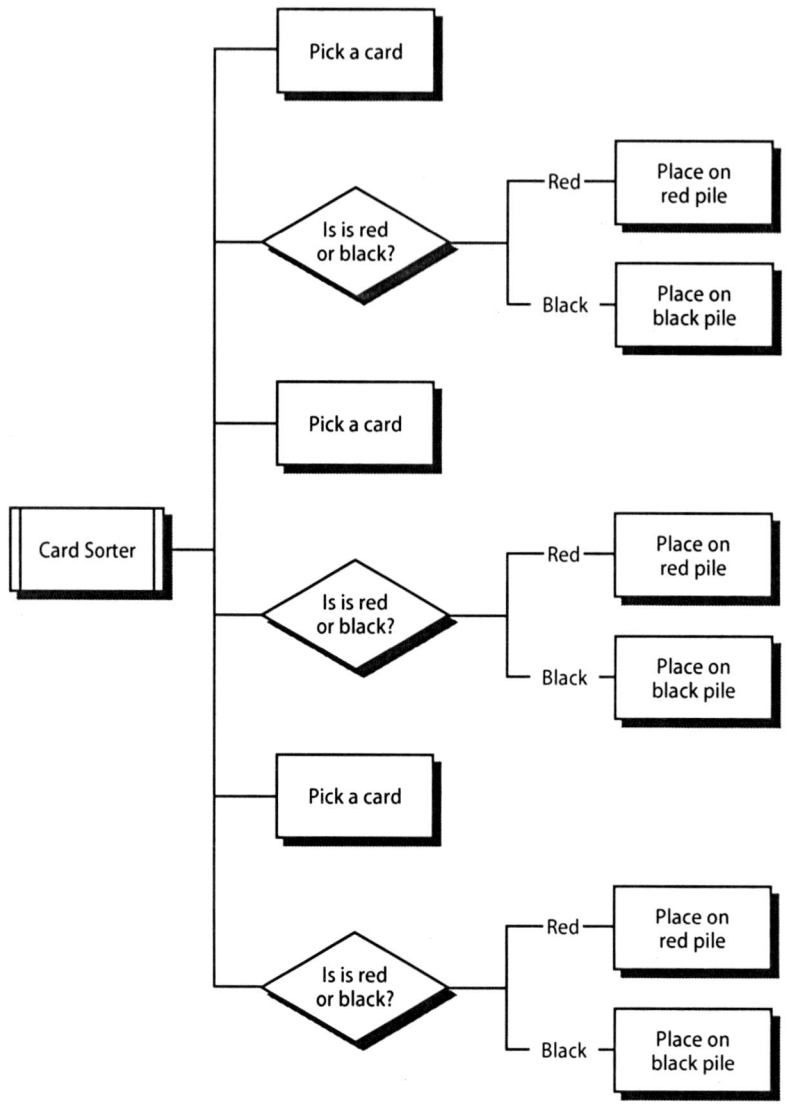

Even for three cards, the diagram is beginning to look big. Imagine what it would look like for all 52 cards in a pack!

A solution to our problem would be to have some way of expressing in the program design (and the program, of course) that we want to perform an action, or a set of actions many times.

In *Chapter Three, page 30*, the loops control structure was introduced. Here is the shape we use:

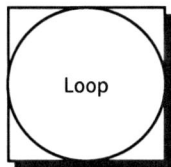

The circle in the box should remind you that we are going round and around!

Here is how we might use a loop in our card game example. We need to pick a card, and place it in the right pile 52 times:

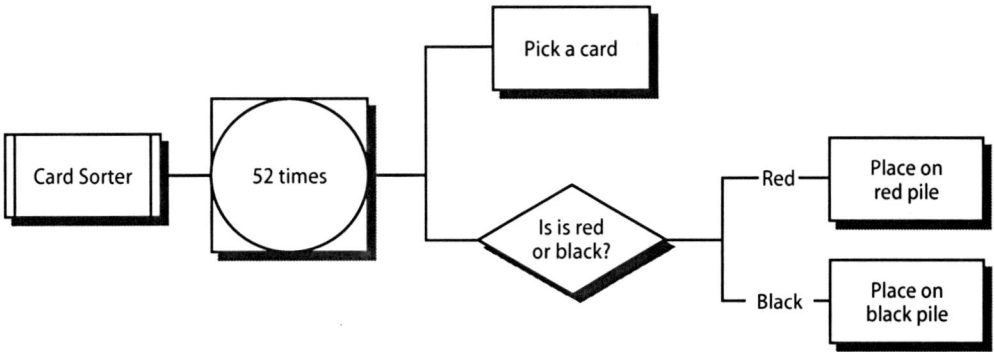

Our new design can be read from left to right:

1. For all 52 cards
    a. pick a card
    b. test for red or black
            i. either place red one on red pile
            ii. or place black one on black pile

Of course, what we need to do now is translate our design into Java. We can do this by using the **for** construct which looks like this:

```
for (Expression1; Expression2; Expression3)
```

We will take each part of this construct and explain what it means:

- Firstly, there is a new keyword, the word **for**.
- **Expression1** is a Java statement, which is executed once and once only to initialise a loop.
- **Expression2** is a Java test condition which is evaluated before we start a loop.
- **Expression3** is a Java statement, which is executed at the end of every time we complete a loop.

The best way to understand how a **for** loop works is by looking at an example. Let's continue with the card game:

```
for (count = 1; count <=52; count++)
{
    System.out.print("Pick a card and input the colour (R or
    B)");
    card = input.next();

    if (card.equals("R"))
        System.out.println("Put it in the reds pile");
    else
        System.out.println("Put it in the blacks pile");
}
```

You should be now be perfectly comfortable with the code that is *inside* the **for** loop (i.e. inside the curly brackets), and hopefully by now, you should be familiar with the indentation of the code, and how it relates to the design chart layout.

Let's concentrate on the new code, specifically this line:

```
for (count = 1; count <=52; count++)
```

As described earlier, there are three expressions inside the round brackets in the line above. Notice how they are separated by semi-colons. Also notice that there is no semi-colon after the third expression, or at the end of the line. We will now analyse each expression:

count = 1;   is a Java statement, which is executed once and once only to initialise a loop. We are using an integer variable, called **count** to help us count through the loop. Its initial value in this case is 1.

count <= 52;   is a Java test condition which is evaluated before we start a loop. It is almost identical to a selection test condition in an **if** clause. Notice however, that the test condition does not have to be in round brackets, and that there is a semi-colon after the condition. The test has two outcomes:

    a. If the test passes, we execute the code *inside* the loop – in our example, if count is less than or equal to 52.

    b. If the test fails, we do not execute the code inside the loop and we continue with the code *after the end of* the loop.

count++   is a Java statement, which is executed at the end of every time we complete a loop. **count++** in Java means **count = count + 1**, and can be read as *increment count*. When we get to the end of a **for** loop, we increment **count**, and start the whole process again.

Let's now return to our example, and go through the code. Here it is again, this time we see the whole program:

```java
import java.util.Scanner;

/* a card game */
class CardSorter
{
   public static void main (String [] args)
   {
       Scanner input = new Scanner(System.in);

       int count; // to keep count of cards
       String card; // for the card colour

       for (count = 1; count <=52; count++)
       {
           System.out.print
                 ("Pick a card and input the colour (R or B)");
           card = input.next();

           if (card.equals("R"))
                 System.out.println("Put it in the reds
                 pile");
           else
                 System.out.println("Put it in the blacks
                 pile");
       }

       System.out.println("THAT'S ALL FOLKS!!!");
   }
}
```

We will start with the line:

```java
for (count = 1; count <=52; count++)
```

Expression1, **count = 1;** is executed first. This is the only time it is executed.

Next, we execute *Expression2*, **count <=52;**, which tests whether count is less than or equal to 52. Of course it is, as count is equal to 1. So the test passes, and we can execute the code inside the loop.

Notice that at this stage, we ignore *Expression3*.

The next line is an opening brace (open curly bracket), which indicates the beginning of the **for** loop.

The following lines of code prompt the user to input the card colour, and a message is output according to that colour. We won't worry too much about this for now. We're only interested in how the **for** loop works.

We know we've hit the end of the **for** loop when we encounter its corresponding closing brace (close curly bracket).

Notice how by using indentation, we can easily see where this is by scanning down the page to look for a close bracket in the same column as its open bracket partner.

This is the point where we execute *Expression3*. Although *Expression3* is written at the top of the loop, remember that it only executes at the end. In our example, **count++** increments **count** from 1 to 2. We've now done everything we need to do in one pass through the loop. The next thing we do is go back to the top of the loop, and start all over again.

So now we are back at the line:

```
for (count = 1; count <=52; count++)
```

Expression1, **count = 1;** is no longer relevant. We executed this once and once only in the first loop.

Next, we execute *Expression2*, **count <=52;**, which tests whether count is less than or equal to 52. We incremented **count** at the end of the first loop, so it is equal to 2. The test passes of course, and we can execute the code inside the loop.

> **NOTE**
>
> Remember, we ignore *Expression3*.

We *go into* the loop again, and ask the user the colour of the card, generating the message according to that colour. When we get to the end of the loop, we execute *Expression3* again, incrementing **count** from 2 to 3. Once we've done this, we go back to the start of the loop, back to the line:

```
for (count = 1; count <=52; count++)
```

Evaluating *Expression2*, **count <=52;** passes again as **count** is equal to 3 now, and we can go on to execute the code inside the loop.

And so the program goes on. By now, you should see the pattern of the loop repeating over and over again, incrementing the counter **count** at the end of each loop. Let's now wind the clock on a bit, and consider what happens towards the end of the loop's *lifetime*, when **count** is eventually equal to 52.

We will assume we're back at the top of the loop, at the line:

```
for (count = 1; count <=52; count++)
```

Evaluating *Expression2*, **count <=52;** passes yet again as **count** is equal to 52. Remember that the test passes if **count** is less than *or equal* to 52. We can go inside the loop (for the last time as we will see) and ask the user for the card colour, etc.

At the end of the loop, as for the previous 51 times, we execute *Expression3*. This time we increment **count** from 52 to 53, then we go back to the top of the loop, to the line:

```
for (count = 1; count <=52; count++)
```

Evaluating *Expression2*, `count <=52;` fails as `count` is equal to 53. The loop is over, R.I.P. loop!! When the test fails, we do not execute the code inside the loop and we continue with the code *after the end of* the loop.

So the next line that executes in the program is the one and only line we haven't dealt with yet, as it features *after* the loop. It also turns out to be the last line in the program:

```
System.out.println("THAT'S ALL FOLKS!!!");
```

DESIGN GUIDELINE

The dry run
We have just stepped through our card program, line by line, to try to establish what the code does. This technique is often called a **dry run,** which means we *ran* through the code (on dry paper), but we didn't actually *run* the program on the computer. A dry run is a very powerful technique for helping you to design, and to a certain extent test, your program logic.

To illustrate how you might perform a dry run in future, let's use an example program:

```
import java.util.Scanner;

/* this program asks five people how they sweeten their
   coffee.
   The three possible answers are: I don't, With sugar, or
   With sweetener. At the end of the program, a report of
   the survey is listed, showing the results */

class CoffeeSurvey
{
    public static void main (String [] args)
    {
        Scanner input = new Scanner(System.in);

        int person, preference, nothing, sugar, sweetener;

        nothing = sugar = sweetener = 0; // set all these to 0
        for (person = 1; person <=5; person++)
        {
            System.out.println("How do you sweeten your
            coffee?");
            System.out.println("1. I don't");
            System.out.println("2. With sugar?");
            System.out.println("3. With sweetener?");

            preference = input.nextInt();

            if (preference == 1)
                  nothing++; // increment it!
```

```
            else if (preference == 2)
                    sugar++;
            else
                    sweetener++;

    }

    System.out.println("Survey Report");
    System.out.println("=============");

    System.out.println(nothing + " people don't sweeten
    coffee");
    System.out.println(sugar + " people use sugar in
    coffee");
    System.out.println(sweetener + " people use sweetener
    in coffee");
    }
}
```

Hopefully, the program is fairly self-explanatory. It simply counts three values, and outputs the results.

To perform a dry run, we begin by drawing a table reserving a column for each variable:

person	preference	nothing	sugar	sweetener

We then go through the program line by line, adding in the values of variables wherever they change. The first line where this happens is:

```
nothing = sugar = sweetener = 0; // set all these to zero
```

This neat technique in Java enables the programmer to set more than one variable to the same value, in this case it's 0. So, in our dry run table:

person	preference	nothing	sugar	sweetener
		0	0	0

The next line is:

```
for (person = 1; person <=5; person++)
```

If you have learnt how the **for** loop works, you'll know that we set person (which will control the person counter) to be equal to 1.

person	preference	nothing	sugar	sweetener
1		0	0	0

We then walk through the code, and ask whether person is less than or equal to 5. It isn't of course, so we go into the loop.

After we prompt the user, we input their preference. Let's assume that the user selects 2, which means they use sugar. In this case, we should increment the sugar variable. We show this in the dry run like this:

person	preference	nothing	sugar	sweetener
1	2	0	0̶	0
			1	

At the end of the loop, we increment the person counter:

person	preference	nothing	sugar	sweetener
1̶	2	0	0̶	0
2			1	

Let's go around again. At the top of the loop, we ask ourselves, is person still less than or equal to 5? It is, so we go in the loop. Let's assume the user types in 3 this time – they like sweetener:

person	preference	nothing	sugar	sweetener
~~1~~	~~2~~	0	~~0~~	~~0~~
2	3		1	1

At the end of the loop, we increment person again:

person	preference	nothing	sugar	sweetener
~~1~~	~~2~~	0	~~0~~	~~0~~
~~2~~	3		1	1
3				

And on we go. The person counter is still less than or equal to 5, so into the loop we go. This time, another person likes sugar:

person	preference	nothing	sugar	sweetener
~~1~~	~~2~~	0	~~0~~	~~0~~
~~2~~	~~3~~		~~1~~	1
3	2		2	

Incrementing the person counter, going into the loop for the fourth time, and preferring nothing in coffee, gives us an updated table which looks like this:

person	preference	nothing	sugar	sweetener
~~1~~	~~2~~	~~0~~	~~0~~	~~0~~
~~2~~	~~3~~	1	~~1~~	1
~~3~~	2		2	
4	1			

Incrementing the person counter this time sets it to 5, which still passes the test as it only fails when it is greater than 5. Let's assume our fifth coffee drinker prefers sugar. Here's the dry run table:

person	preference	nothing	sugar	sweetener
~~1~~	~~2~~	~~0~~	~~0~~	~~0~~
~~2~~	~~3~~	1	~~1~~	1
~~3~~	~~2~~		~~2~~	
~~4~~	~~1~~		3	
5	2			

When we get to the end of the loop this time, we increment the person counter to 6:

person	preference	nothing	sugar	sweetener
~~1~~	~~2~~	~~0~~	~~0~~	~~0~~
~~2~~	~~3~~	1	~~1~~	1
~~3~~	~~2~~		~~2~~	
~~4~~	~~1~~		3	
~~5~~	2			
6				

Going back to the top of the loop, we realise now that our test fails, as the person counter is no longer less than or equal to 5. The program should now produce its report, listing the correct final values for the three coffee tastes. It should tell us that one person likes plain coffee, three like sugar, and one likes sweetener.

Your dry run should give you the confidence that when you type in, compile and run your program, it will provide the same results in the *actual run* as those in your *dry run*.

DESIGN GUIDELINE

Move on, print off, and chill out...

Conducting a dry run is extremely useful when your program doesn't do what you think it should. It may *work* – that is to say it doesn't give any compilation errors, but it may not give the results you expect. Dry runs can often show you where things are going wrong.

A good idea when you are frustrated with your program is to print off a copy of your source code, move well away from the computer to a more comfortable place (have a drink, try to calm down), and dry run your code from the source code listing. A friend or colleague might be able to help in this process too. Experience shows that following this guideline will save you a lot of time (and your blood pressure!) in the long run.

More for loop examples

We have seen that there are three expressions in a **for** loop. As long as we conform to the rules of Java, we can produce many variations of **for** loops, and we can use them in very powerful ways. We don't have to start with a counter of one for example, and we don't have to step in sequences of one. We can also count down as well as up, and we can test for complex conditions. Here are some further examples of **for** loops:

```
// count from 1 to whatever the variable noOfStudents holds
for (student = 1; student<= noOfStudents; student++)


// start a maximum salary rate and count down to the minimum
// salaryRate-- means decrement salaryRate
for (salaryRate = maxRate; salaryRate>= minRate; salaryRate--)
```

```
// count in steps of two
// for expression 3, you could also use count+=2 for shorthand!
for (count = 1; count < 30; count = count + 2)
```

Exercise 5.1: More coffee

In the coffee survey program, what would happen if **nothing, sugar** and **sweetener** were not originally set to zero? Would the program work?

▶ Create the coffee survey program and get it working.

▶ Test to see what happens when only one person likes a particular way of drinking coffee?

▶ Modify your program to report in correct English by stating "Only 1 person … " rather than "1 people …".

▶ Modify the coffee survey program to validate the three choices.

▶ Trap for out of range values (i.e. where the user types in a number other than 1, 2, or 3). **Make sure your program still processes 5 valid selections.**

Exercise 5.2: Square and cube

▶ Design, write, and test a program to input seven integers and, for each integer, calculate and display its square and cube.

Exercise 5.3: Payslips

▶ Design, write, and test a program to input five pairs of numbers, the first number representing hours worked and the second number representing rate of pay per hour for each of five workers. For each worker, calculate and output the gross pay earned.

Exercise 5.4: Commission

▶ Design, write, and test a program to input the commission figures for ten sales staff; calculate and output the total commission overall and the average commission.

Exercise 5.5: Student marks

 Design, write, and test a program to input the number of students sitting an examination, followed by an exam mark for each of the students. For each student, display the mark and a message "Pass" or "Fail", depending on whether the mark is at least 40 (for a Pass) or less than 40 (for a Fail).

Exercise 5.6: Multiplication table

 Input an integer between 1 and 100 and output the multiplication table for that integer, i.e.:

$$1 \text{ X integer} = ?$$
$$2 \text{ X integer} = ?$$

....

$$12 \text{ X integer} = ?.$$

More loops

So far, we have seen the **for** loop, and how we can execute the same piece of code a given number of times. The **for** loop counts from an initial value, checks whether the value is in a range, and updates the value at the end of the loop. Basically, it is a counter – it counts its way up, down, or however the programmer has programmed it. A key thing to notice about the **for** loop is that we should know *before the for loop begins*, how many times we want to repeat the loop. In the case of the card game, it was 52 times, in the case of the coffee survey, it was 5, in this case:

```
// count from 1 to whatever the variable noOfStudents holds

for (student = 1; student<= noOfStudents; student++)
```

it is **noOfStudents** times (this variable must have a value *before the for loop begins*).

> **NOTE**
>
> The for loop is very powerful for counting through a loop, but it is not so good if we don't know in advance of hitting the loop how many times we will go through it.

Consider the following examples:

- process all today's invoices until there are none left;

- take an order for a drink, then the next one, and the next, and so on;

- move an enemy spaceship around the screen in a computer game until it gets shot down;

- charge 20 pence per minute for a phone call until the caller hangs up;

- show a menu on a cash machine screen until the user asks for their card back.

In fact, most computer programs involve something being done an unknown number of times. Of course, as this is such an important thing to do in programming, Java has a special construct for this. It is called the **while loop**.

Before we introduce the **while** loop, here is a bit of revision. Remember the **if** clause? Here's an example:

```
if (preference != 4)
```

This reads *if the variable called preference is not equal to 4*. The **if** clause has a keyword **if** and a test condition (the stuff in round brackets). The reason why we show you this again is because the **while** loop follows EXACTLY the same pattern:

```
while (preference != 4)
```

Instead of the **if** keyword, we have a new keyword **while**. The rest is the same. We have a test condition in round brackets. The **while** loop works in the same way too, **EXCEPT** that we repeat the code *inside* the loop *over and over again* until the test fails.

Here is an example program, which uses a **while** loop:

```java
import java.util.Scanner;

/* this program asks people how they sweeten their coffee.
   The three possible answers are: I don't, With sugar, or
   With sweetener. At the end of the program, a report of
   the survey is listed, showing the results */

class AnotherCoffeeSurvey
{
    public static void main (String [] args)
    {
        Scanner input = new Scanner(System.in);

        int preference, nothing, sugar, sweetener;

        nothing = sugar = sweetener = 0;/* set all these to
        zero */

        // ask about the first person
        System.out.println("How do you sweeten your
        coffee?");
        System.out.println("1. I don't");
        System.out.println("2. With sugar?");
        System.out.println("3. With sweetener?");
        System.out.println("4. Quit");

        preference = input.nextInt();

        while (preference != 4)
```

```
        {
            if (preference == 1)
                    nothing++; // increment it!
            else if (preference == 2)
                    sugar++;
            else
                    sweetener++;

            // ask about the next person
            System.out.println("How do you sweeten your
            coffee?");
            System.out.println("1. I don't");
            System.out.println("2. With sugar?");
            System.out.println("3. With sweetener?");
            System.out.println("4. Quit");

            preference = input.nextInt();
        }

        System.out.println("Survey Report");
        System.out.println("=============");

        System.out.println(nothing + " people don't sweeten
        coffee");
        System.out.println(sugar + " people use sugar in
        coffee");
        System.out.println(sweetener + " people use sweetener
        in coffee");
    }
}
```

You will surely recognise parts of the program above. It is very similar to the coffee survey example where we used a **for** loop. This time we use a **while** loop, because we don't know how many people will take part in the survey.

We will now discuss the differences between the **for** loop and the **while** loop.

1. we use the **while** clause instead of the **for** clause (obviously);

2. the **while** clause has one thing inside the round brackets (a test condition), whereas the **for** clause has three things;

3. the two things that the **while** loop is missing give an initial value for the test condition (*expression1*), and an updated new value to test for the next time around the loop (*expression3*).

Let's look at the third difference more closely. As we know, *expression1* in the **for** clause executes once and only once at the very start of the loop. It provides an initial value for *expression2* (the test condition) to test.

In a **while** loop, we still need an initial value for the test condition to test. We do this by making sure that we provide that initial value *before we get to the loop*. If you look at our new coffee survey, you can see that this is done by asking the first user their coffee preference. We also give the option to quit the program (option 4). Notice how we no longer need to ask the question immediately after the start of the loop (as we did in the **for** loop).

Remember *expression3* in the **for** clause, which executes at the end of the loop, and updates the value we test for the next time around? As we now know, we don't have this in a **while** loop, but we still need to make sure we get a new value to test for the next time around the loop. In our coffee survey example, we do this by asking the next user their coffee preference *just before the end of the loop*. In fact, we have used exactly the same code here as we used just before we started the loop. This idea is a very important design guideline for **while** loops. It is called **read ahead**.

```
C:\WINDOWS\system32\cmd.exe

C:\Java>javac AnotherCoffeeSurvey.java

C:\Java>java AnotherCoffeeSurvey
How do you sweeten your coffee?
1. I don't
2. With sugar?
3. With sweetener?
4. Quit
1
How do you sweeten your coffee?
1. I don't
2. With sugar?
3. With sweetener?
4. Quit
2
How do you sweeten your coffee?
1. I don't
2. With sugar?
3. With sweetener?
4. Quit
3
How do you sweeten your coffee?
1. I don't
2. With sugar?
3. With sweetener?
4. Quit
4
Survey Report
=============
1 people don't sweeten coffee
1 people use sugar in coffee
1 people use sweetener in coffee

C:\Java>
```

DESIGN GUIDELINE

ALWAYS use read ahead with while loops

The **read ahead** is crucial because it makes the **while** loop a lot easier to control. Read ahead basically means that we read (input) a value ahead (before) we get to the loop. It is a very easy thing to implement as it follows a simple pattern – you just have to remember to do it!

Let's consider the **read ahead** pattern by looking at its design:

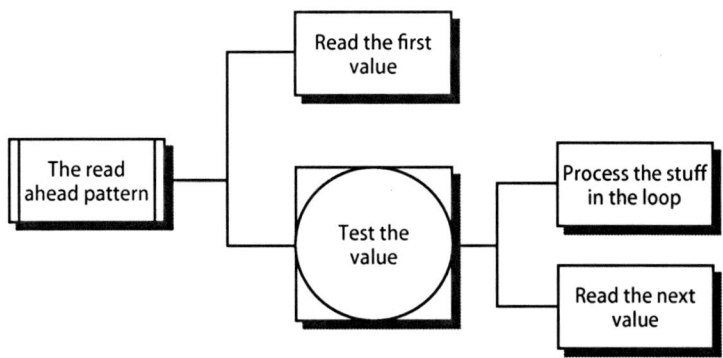

Following this design, we have the following sequence of events:

> Read the first value
>
> Test the value
>
> Process the stuff in the loop
>
> Read the next value
>
> Test the value
>
> Process the stuff in the loop
>
> Read the next value
>
> Test the value
>
> Process the stuff in the loop
>
> Read the next value
>
>
> and so on until the test fails, so the last time we have:
>
>
> Test the value
>
> Process the stuff in the loop
>
> Read the next value
>
> Test the value
>
>
> and finish

Notice that we have a sequence of read, test, process, read, test, process, read, test – the first thing we do is read (that's why we call it read ahead, of course), and the last thing we do is test – just like we do in a different way with the **for** loop.

To compare how we design using a **for** loop and a **while** loop, here are the two designs for our alternative coffee survey programs. Notice how we use the same box for a **for** and a **while** loop, but see where the reading of values differs.

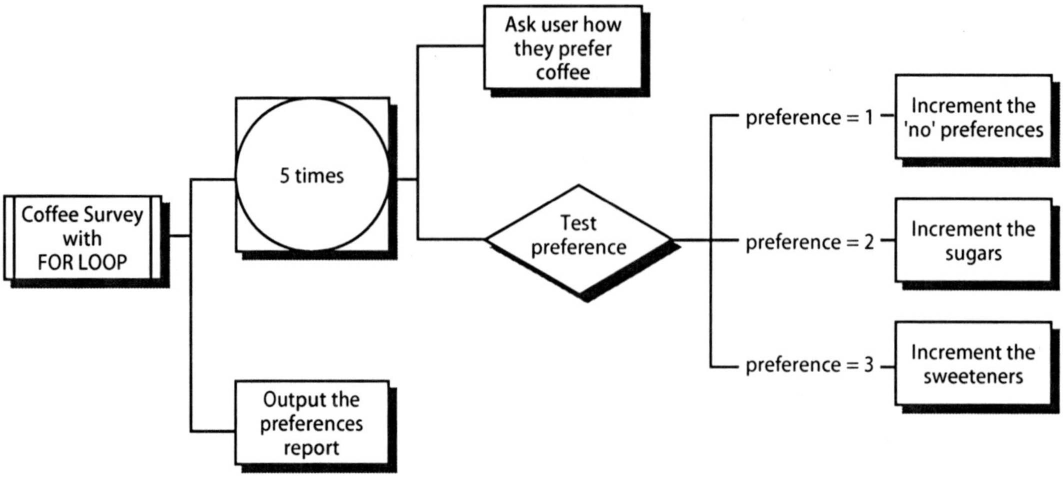

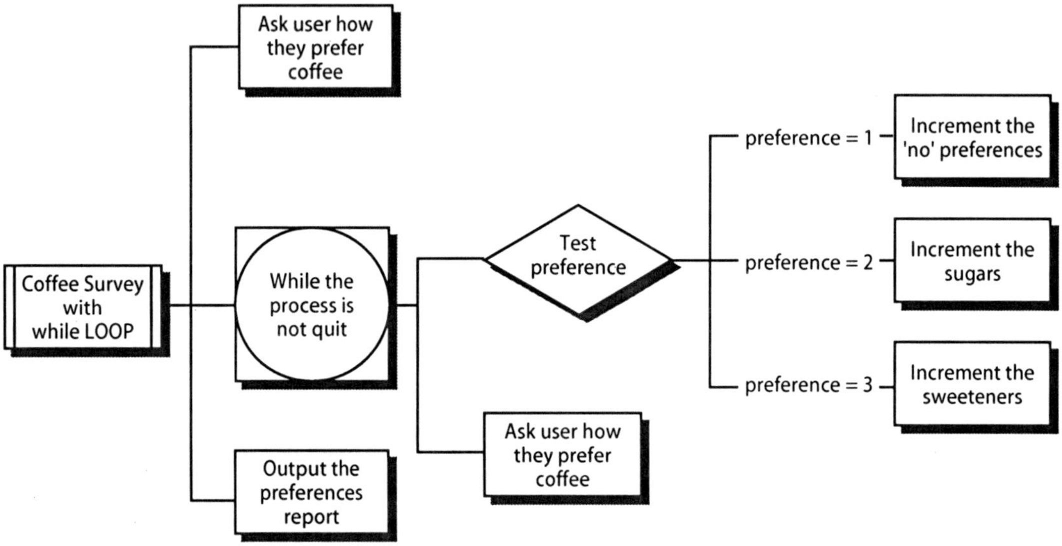

Coffee Survey with FOR LOOP

- 5 times
  - Ask user how they prefer coffee
  - Test preference
    - preference = 1 — Increment the 'no' preferences
    - preference = 2 — Increment the sugars
    - preference = 3 — Increment the sweeteners
- Output the preferences report

Coffee Survey with while LOOP

- Ask user how they prefer coffee
- While the process is not quit
  - Test preference
    - preference = 1 — Increment the 'no' preferences
    - preference = 2 — Increment the sugars
    - preference = 3 — Increment the sweeteners
  - Ask user how they prefer coffee
- Output the preferences report

Exercise 5.7: Even more coffee

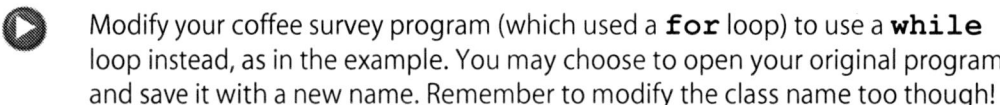 Modify your coffee survey program (which used a **for** loop) to use a **while** loop instead, as in the example. You may choose to open your original program and save it with a new name. Remember to modify the class name too though!

A new requirement for the program is to output the number of people surveyed in the report. Use a new variable called **personCount** to do this, which you should update every time you run through the loop.

Exercise 5.9: More student marks

▶ Design, write and test a program to input student marks in a test. Output 'Pass' if the mark is 40 or above, otherwise output 'Fail'. Input a mark of -1 to finish the program.

▶ Modify the design and the code of the above program to output the number of students who took the test, the number of passes, the number of fails, and the overall average mark.

▶ What happens in the above program if there are no students? Make sure your program can cope with zero or more students.

Exercise 5.10: Payroll

▶ Design, write and test a program to process a payroll. You should input the employee name, their hourly rate, and the number of hours each employee has worked. Output the gross pay and the net pay (with a tax rate of 30%). When there are no more employees, input the word "End", instead of the employee name.

Exercise 5.11: Higher or lower?

▶ A simple two player game involves player 1 typing in a number, and player 2 guessing the number. Each time player 2 guesses the wrong answer, the computer must reply "Try higher" or "Try lower", to give the player a clue for the next try. When the correct number is guessed, the number of guesses taken will be output, and the program will end. Design and write a program to play the guessing game.

Exercise 5.12: Module marks

▶ Design, write and test a program to process student module marks. The input data for each student consists of their name, followed by a group of 6 marks for each student (e.g. 56, 45, 75, 32, 68, 39). For each student, calculate the average mark and print a result depending on this average – "Pass" if at least 40, otherwise "Fail". The program finishes when the user types "End" when prompted for the student's name. Your program should process any number of students.

Java Forum

Post	**My for loop won't compile – why not?** ⭐
Reply	A common mistake with programming **for** loops is where a comma is used to separate the three expressions. Remember – use a semi-colon to separate the three expressions in a **for** loop. ☺

Post	**My program has gone crazy. HELP!!!** ⭐
Reply	Writing programs with loops can be a traumatic experience. If your program seems to go crazy when you run it, you are most probably *stuck* in what we call an *infinite loop*. This happens when there is no way out of the loop for the program, so it just keeps repeating forever. They almost always happen in **while** loops. The three common causes of infinite loops are:

1. Where a **while** loop has no update of the test value in it, so the test condition never fails. For example, you may have forgotten the read ahead at the beginning or end of the loop, .

2. Where a single equals is used in a **while** loop test condition. **ALWAYS** use a double equals sign when testing for equivalence.

3. Where a semi-colon is placed at the end of the **while** clause, like this:

```
/* the semi-colon ends the while loop so goes
around forever */
while ( !name.equals("End") );
```
☺

Post	**How do I test a loop?** ⭐
Reply	Testing loops can be a problem, especially with **while** loops, as potentially the loop could last forever, and it would take that long to test for an infinite number of passes through the loop. That would be impossible of course, so choosing a sensible subset of tests is a good idea. As a general guideline, test for at least five passes through the loop, and add to this every possible path through the program. For example, there are four paths through the coffee survey **while** loop program. There are three conditions (nothing, sugar, and sweetener), AND one more – where there are NO PEOPLE in the survey – that is to say that the user quits without anyone taking part in the survey. It is important to test for

this case of zero passes. So for the coffee program, five + four, equalling nine is a reasonable number of passes through the loop to test for. You can use your design chart to analyse how many possible routes there are through your program.
☺

You will have noticed that using read ahead requires you to duplicate code. You can also see the duplication in the design. Here's a reminder, using the coffee survey once more:

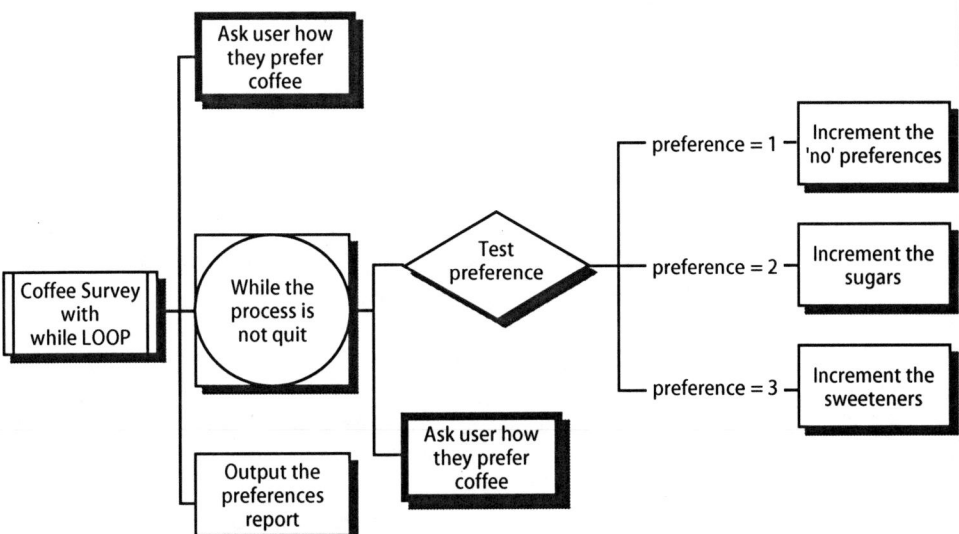

The boxes in thick lines indicate the duplication. In the program itself, we duplicate the following lines, which display the menu of choices to the user:

```
System.out.println("How do you sweeten your coffee?");
System.out.println("1. I don't");
System.out.println("2. With sugar?");
System.out.println("3. With sweetener?");
System.out.println("4. Quit");
```

Of course, it is a bit of a pain to duplicate the code, and it's also dangerous. What if we changed the menu? We'd have to remember to change two areas of the program!

A good way around this is to use a Java **method**. A method is a collection of Java code that can be used several times in a program.

Here is an example of a method – we will continue with the coffee survey example:

```
public static void menu ()
{
    System.out.println("How do you sweeten your coffee?");
    System.out.println("1. I don't");
    System.out.println("2. With sugar?");
    System.out.println("3. With sweetener?");
    System.out.println("4. Quit");
}
```

We name our methods in the same way we do variables. We've called our method **menu** in this case. You may notice that the rest of the line where we name the method follows a very similar pattern to the line that looks like this in ALL your programs:

```
public static void main (String [] args)
```

This line declares the **main** method, and must feature in **EVERY** Java program. The **main** method always runs first in a Java program, but this method can call up other methods to ask them to do some work.

More on methods later, but as a taster, here's how we would put the program together. Notice where the **main** method calls the **menu** method, and where in the program the two methods reside.

```
import java.util.Scanner;

/* this program asks people how they sweeten their
   coffee. The three possible answers are: I don't,
   With sugar, or With sweetener. At the end of the
   program, a report of the survey is listed, showing
   the results */

class AnotherCoffeeSurvey
{
    public static void menu ()
    {
        System.out.println("How do you sweeten your
        coffee?");
        System.out.println("1. I don't");
        System.out.println("2. With sugar?");
        System.out.println("3. With sweetener?");
        System.out.println("4. Quit");
    }
```

```
public static void main (String [] args)
{
    Scanner input = new Scanner(System.in);

    int preference, nothing, sugar, sweetener;

    nothing = sugar = sweetener = 0; /* set all
    these to zero */

    // ask about the first person
    menu();

    preference = input.nextInt();

    while (preference != 4)
    {
        if (preference == 1)
                nothing++; // increment it!
        else if (preference == 2)
                sugar++;
        else
                sweetener++;

        // ask about the next person
        menu();

        preference = input.nextInt();
    }

    System.out.println("Survey Report");
    System.out.println("=============");

    System.out.println(nothing + " people don't
    sweeten coffee");
    System.out.println(sugar + " people use sugar in
    coffee");
    System.out.println(sweetener + " people use
    sweetener in coffee");
    }
}
```

☺

Chapter 6

SUB-PROGRAMS

Chapter overview

In the previous chapter on loops, we introduced Java methods. The Java method helped us to overcome the duplication problem we had with the read-only technique we used for the **while** loop. In the **AnotherCoffeeSurvey** program, we used two methods: the **main** method (which must be in every Java program) and the **menu** method (which we created ourselves). Java methods can be termed **sub-programs**, as we can use many of them to create one larger program. As we have seen, they help us deal with duplication, but they are also extremely useful for other reasons:

- they make programs easier to read;

- they make programs easier to change or modify;

- they make programs more reliable;

- they make programs easier to design;

- they allow many people to work on the same program or system.

Put together, these reasons provide a very powerful argument for using sub-programs wherever possible. The aim of this chapter is to convince you that learning to program with sub-programs is essential.

At the end of this chapter you will be able to:

- break down a difficult problem into a set of smaller, more manageable ones;

- design and write programs that use several Java methods;

- send messages in the form of data between methods.

Problem solving made easy

To illustrate the principle of sub-programs, let's consider this real-world problem:

How do I get from the train station to the library?

If a stranger asked you this question outside the train station, you'd no doubt give them some simple directions, for example:

1.   turn left at the top of the road;

2.   walk down the hill to the traffic lights;

3.   turn right and keep going until you get to the square;

4.   the library is on your right.

Here, the stranger has been given four instructions. It looks like they need to do four different things to solve the problem of getting to the library. However, of course they will need to do a lot more than four things to get to the library. They'll need to refine each of the instructions and break them down into smaller ones. For example, for instruction 1, there may be some other, more detailed problems to solve:

1.   Turn left at the top of the road:

    a.   walk to the train station entrance;

    b.   look for the top of the road;

    c.   walk in a straight line avoiding obstacles;

    d.   stop at the top of the road;

    e.   turn left.

Taking things to a seemingly ridiculous level, we could go even further:

1.   turn left at the top of the road;

    a.   walk to the train station entrance:

        i.   left;

        ii.   right;

        iii.   left;

        iv.   right;

        v.   left;

        vi.   right;

        vii.   push door open;

        viii. left;

        ix.   right;

        x.   left;

        xi.   right;

        xii.   stop.

In fact, we could go further still if we wanted to include breathing, blinking, arm movements, finger movements etc. Of course, we don't think about any of this in real-life, but it is interesting to note that if this was a computer game with characters moving around in a simulated world, we would have to consider character movement in intricate detail. To do this for every move, for every character, in every situation would be a daunting task. If we use sub-programs, it would be a lot easier.

Another thing to observe here is that by breaking the directions and associated moves into sub-problems (starting with the initial four instructions), it was a lot easier to describe. The technique we used was stepwise refinement, just like in the program designs we have already done.

Using our graphical notation, we could design a program to walk a character to the destination:

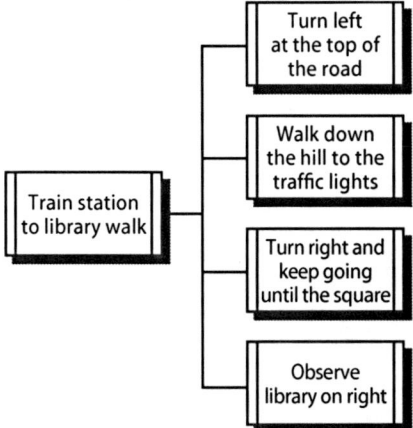

Notice that all the boxes in the above diagram use the notation:

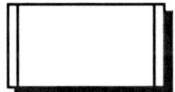

We use this box wherever we use a sub-program, or in Java terminology, a **method**. We design our sub-programs separately, for example:

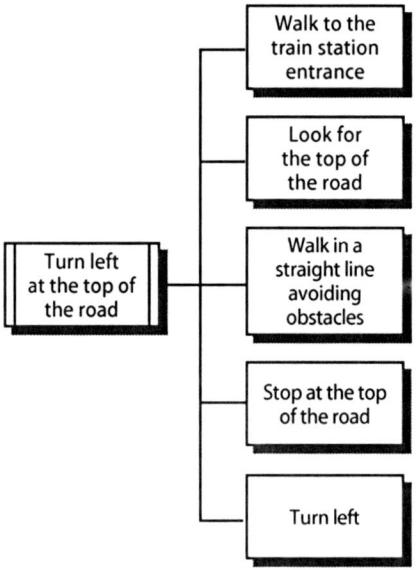

In this way, we could have a number of programmers working on the same program, but working individually on the various sub-programs.

Programming with methods

Writing graphical computer games is a very advanced form of programming, and is beyond the scope of this book. However, we can use some simple programming techniques to perform some trivial animation. Let's consider a program specification:

A character is seven steps from a wall. Move the character towards the wall by repeatedly typing any key, followed by the enter key. When the character hits the wall, output the message: "OUCH!". Use a "k" for the character and a "I--I" string for the wall.

Because of the graphical limitations of our programming, we will produce a very clumsy looking animation, which should look something like this:

```
k         I--I
 k        I--I
  k       I--I
   k      I--I
    k     I--I
     k  I--I
      kI--I
   OUCH!
```

We can deal with the animation by outputting a number of spaces before the character and a number of spaces after the character, before we output the wall string. As the character gets nearer the wall, the number of spaces before increases from zero to seven, and the number of spaces after decreases from seven down to zero. If we used a for loop to count the seven steps, with a counter called step, before the character we would always print step number of spaces, and after the character, we would always print 7-step number of spaces.

Here's our design for the program:

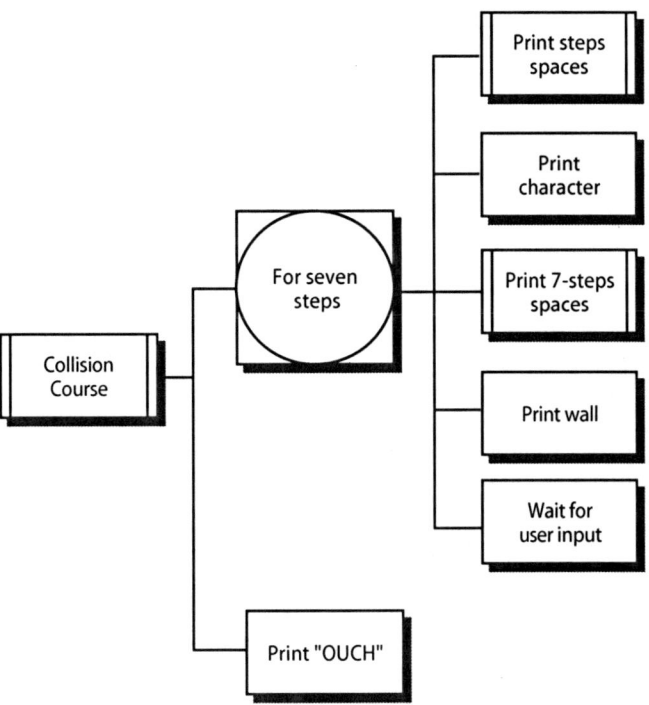

> **NOTE**
>
> Notice how we have two sub-program boxes in our design. However, because sub-programs are very powerful and flexible, we will see that we only need to write one Java method to solve this problem. We can do this by sending the method the number of spaces it needs to print.

This works just like sending an e-mail, or a mobile phone text message to use another example, in the real world. When you send someone a message, it usually has some information in it. When you call a method in Java, it can have information in it too. In programming, we call this kind of information **input parameters**.

Just like in real-world e-mail or text messaging where you can reply to the message sender, a method can reply to its caller. Information that is sent back to the calling method (in our case the main method) is called a **return parameter** or an **output parameter**. At the moment, we will only deal with input parameters. Output parameters will be described later in the chapter.

Let's now look at the code for the main method. We don't need to worry about the sub-program yet.

```
public static void main(String[] args)
{
    Scanner input = new Scanner(System.in);

    int step;
    String walk;

    // seven steps overall
    for (step = 1; step <= 7; step++)
    {
        // spaces before, starting from 1 and going up
        outputSpaces(step);

        System.out.print("k");

        // spaces after, starting from 7 and going down
        outputSpaces(7 - step);

        System.out.print("I--I");

        walk = input.next();
    }

    System.out.print("OUCH!");
}
```

Notice how we call our method, which is named **outputSpaces**. When we called the **menu** method in the previous chapter, we wrote it like this:

```
menu();
```

The open and close brackets contain nothing. This is called a **void** method, because we don't send any data (parameters) to the method we are calling. However, with our new method **outputSpaces**, we send a number to the method to tell it how many spaces we'd like it to print. This number is enclosed in the brackets, like this:

```
outputSpaces(step);
```

and this:

```
outputSpaces(7 - step);
```

> **NOTE**
>
> As long as the value in brackets evaluates to an integer, it will be a valid parameter to send to the method.

We call the method twice in the loop, each time with a different number, which relates directly to the counter variable in the loop, which is named **step**. The loop executes seven times, so **outputSpaces** is called a total of 14 times.

> **NOTE**
>
> Notice at this point, we still don't know what the **outputSpaces** method looks like. All we know is that we plan to send it an input parameter, which is an integer. Hopefully, you will now see the power not only of using sub-programs, but also the design technique of stepwise refinement, which we've been using ever since we began our design work.

Once we are satisfied with the design of the main method, we can concentrate on thinking about the design of the new method. We want the method to print a variable number of spaces, so it makes sense to use a loop to do this. A simple design for the method is shown below:

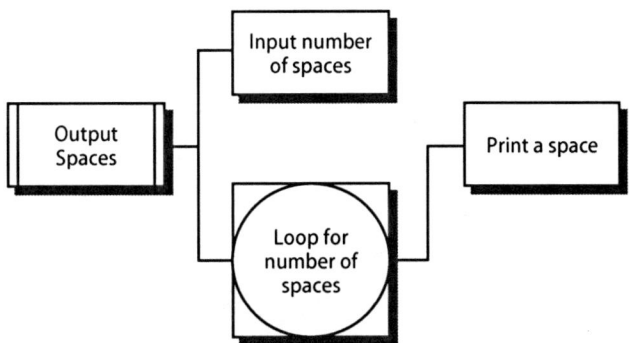

Notice that we have a box called **input number of spaces**. So far, whenever we have input anything, it has come from the user – typing in a number, for example. In this case however, the number is not being input by the user. Rather it is provided by the calling method. The **main** method sends the value to **outputSpaces** as an input parameter. How we code this is completely different from coding user input, as can be seen from the Java code below:

```java
public static void outputSpaces(int howMany)
{
    for (int spaces = 1; spaces <= howMany; spaces++)
        System.out.print(" ");
}
```

We will discuss the **outputSpaces** method carefully, starting with the first line:

```java
public static void outputSpaces(int howMany)
```

This line of code is where we declare the `outputSpaces` method. It is declared in much the same way as the `main` method, but with some differences. The first three words, `public static void` are the same. The fourth word `outputSpaces` is quite clearly the name of the method. As long as you conform to Java naming conventions, you can call a method whatever you like. We know it's called `outputSpaces` because we need to use its name when we call it from the `main` method.

Now onto the contents of the brackets:

```
(int howMany)
```

The contents of the brackets should remind you of how we declare a variable in Java. In fact, that is exactly what we are doing. We are declaring an integer variable called **howMany** which will be assigned the value that is passed to the **outputSpaces** method by the calling method. This value can obviously be different every time the method is called. One important thing to note is that the type of variable declared in the brackets must be of the same type as that which is sent to it. In our case here, they are both integers. We will see later that we can use any number of parameters in a method, not just one (or zero as in the case of a void method).

Here's the next line of code:

```
for (int spaces = 1; spaces <= howMany; spaces++)
```

The loop uses a new integer variable called **spaces**. Notice that we have declared the variable in the same line as the **for** loop. We can do this in Java. We can declare variables effectively wherever we like. However, where we declare them dictates where we can use them. **spaces** can only be used in the **for** loop, because that is where we declared it. **howMany** can only be used in **outputSpaces**, because that is where we declared it. **step** and **walk** can only be used in the main method, because that is where we declared them.

This is a very powerful feature of Java, as it allows variables to be **localised** to sections of the program. If a variable could be used anywhere in a program, its value could be very difficult to keep track of, especially in a large program. We use the term **local variable** for variables which are known only to the method where they are declared.

Finally, we have the line:

```
System.out.print(" ");
```

which prints out a single space. Notice we use **print**, not **println**, as we don't want the cursor to move on to the next line after a space is printed.

Once the loop has finished we reach the end of the **outputSpaces** method. Control is then returned to the calling method, which resumes from where it left off.

Putting the two methods together gives us the whole program:

```java
import java.util.Scanner;

/* A character is seven steps from a wall. Move the character
   towards the wall by repeatedly typing a character and
   hitting the enter key.
   When the character hits the wall, output the message:
   "Ouch!". Use a "k" for the character and a "I--I" string
   for the wall. */

class CollisionCourse
{
   public static void outputSpaces(int howMany)
   {
      for (int spaces = 1; spaces <= howMany; spaces++)
         System.out.print(" ");

   }

   public static void main(String[] args)
   {
      Scanner input = new Scanner(System.in);

      int step;
      String walk;

      // seven steps overall
      for (step = 1; step <= 7; step++)
      {
         /* spaces before the character, starting from 1
         and going up */
         outputSpaces(step);

         System.out.print("k");

         /* spaces after the character, starting from 7,
         going down */
         outputSpaces(7 - step);

         System.out.print("I--I");

         walk = input.next();
      }

      System.out.print("OUCH!");
   }
}
```

```
C:\WINDOWS\system32\cmd.exe

C:\Java>javac CollisionCourse.java

C:\Java>java CollisionCourse
 k        I--I.
  k       I--I.
   k      I--I.
    k     I--I.
     k   I--I.
      k I--I.
       kI--I.
OUCH!
C:\Java>_
```

More methods

Now we will make our animation better by simulating the character moving along the screen more realistically. The solution we have so far displays the character's new position on a new line. We can improve this by clearing the screen every time we redraw the picture of the character and the wall. We will do this by writing a simple method which prints a series of new lines to wipe the contents of the screen. We will assume that the screen has 25 lines:

```
public static void clearScreen()
{
    for (int line = 1; line <= 25; line++)
        System.out.println();
}
```

Our method is called **clearScreen** and has no input parameter. It is a **void** function. We know we're going to print 25 lines every time the method is called, so we don't need any information from outside the method itself.

We can now put this method in our program. We will call **clearScreen** from the **main** method every time we go around the loop.

Here is the new program:

```java
import java.util.Scanner;

/* A character is seven steps from a wall. Move the
character towards the wall by repeatedly typing a character
and hitting the enter key.When the character hits the wall,
output the message: "Ouch!". Use a "k" for the character and
a "I--I" string for the wall. */
class CollisionCourse
{
   public static void clearScreen()
   {
      for (int line = 1; line <= 25; line++)
         System.out.println();
   }
   public static void outputSpaces(int howMany)
   {
      for (int spaces = 1; spaces <= howMany; spaces++)
         System.out.print(" ");
   }
   public static void main(String[] args)
   {
      Scanner input = new Scanner(System.in);
      int step;
      String walk;
      // seven steps overall
      for (step = 1; step <= 7; step++)
      {
         clearScreen();

         /* spaces before the character, starting from 1
         and going up */
         outputSpaces(step);

         System.out.print("k");

         /* spaces after the character, starting from 7,
         going down */
         outputSpaces(7 - step);

         System.out.print("I--I");

         walk = input.next();
      }

      System.out.print("OUCH!");
   }
}
```

Exercise 6.1: Hello again

 Design, build and test a program that asks the user to input a number, and output the message "Hello world" that number of times. Your program must have a separate method which outputs the set of messages.

More parameters

In this section, we'll look at more things we can do with input and output parameters. We will see examples of methods that use several parameters, and will explain how to work with them, starting with **return parameters**.

The return parameter

Earlier, we mentioned that methods work a little like text messages on mobile phones. When we are called we get a message, and we can then reply to that message if we want to. We can do this in Java very simply, by using a **return parameter**.

Let's consider an example:

> Design and build a program which doubles the number input by the user and outputs the result. Write a method called **doubleIt** to perform the calculation.

By now, you should immediately realise that the problem to be solved here is very simple – it follows the basic input, process, output pattern. The only difference here is that we have to use a method to perform the process phase of the program. Here is the design for the main method:

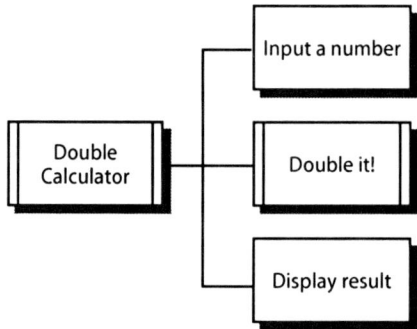

The new method **doubleIt** will take a single parameter as its input. However, it needs to reply to the main method, sending back a value equivalent to double the number it received. The value it sends back is called a return parameter. Here is the design for the **doubleIt** method:

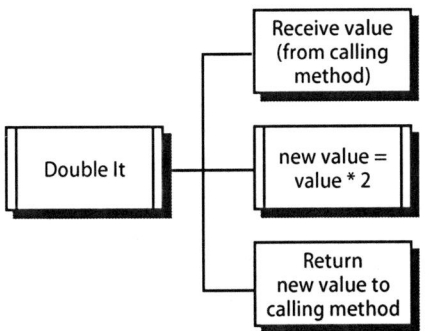

As you can see, **doubleIt** also follows the input, process, output pattern. However, the input is now received from the calling method, not the user (just like the **outputSpaces** method). Nor is the output displayed to the user. Rather, it is now returned to the calling method.

Here is the Java code for the **doubleIt** method:

```
public static int doubleIt(int value)
{
    int newValue;

    newValue = value * 2;

    return newValue;
}
```

We will now discuss the method, line by line, starting with the first line:

```
public static int doubleIt(int value)
```

You should now be familiar with the way the input parameter **value** works, as it behaves exactly the same way that **howMany** worked in the **outputSpaces** method. The major difference between **doubleIt** and **ALL** the other methods you've seen so far is that we no longer use the word **void** in the method declaration. We have replaced that word here with the word **int**.

The reason we have done this is that the word immediately after **public static** in a method declaration describes what is sent back (returned) from that method whenever it is called. Every method we've used in the past returns nothing, and this is why the word **void** is used (which means empty, of course).

Our new method **doubleIt** returns something though. In the method declaration, we must specify what type of something we are returning. In this case, we are returning an integer, so we use the keyword **int**.

The next line is a variable declaration:

```
int newValue;
```

We will use this variable to store the doubled value sent to us by the **main** method, and we perform the calculation itself in the next line:

```
newValue = value * 2;
```

The final line introduces a new keyword, **return**.

```
return newValue;
```

This line simply returns the value it refers to (in this case **newValue**) back to the calling method.

Now we will look at the whole program:

```
import java.util.Scanner;

/* Design and build a program which doubles the number input
   by the user and outputs the result.  */

class DoubleCalc
{
   public static int doubleIt(int value)
   {
      int newValue;

      newValue = value * 2;

      return newValue;
   }

   public static void main(String[] args)
   {
      Scanner input = new Scanner(System.in);

      int number, result;

      System.out.print("Input a number ");
      number = input.nextInt();

      // now call the doubleIt method
      result = doubleIt(number);

      System.out.print("The result is " + result);
   }
}
```

Notice how **doubleIt** is called from the **main** method. The **main** method sends the value of **number** to **doubleIt**. The value of **number** is copied into the variable **value** inside the **doubleIt** method. When **doubleIt** runs, it passes back **newValue** to the **main** method when the return statement is executed. This value is then assigned to the variable **result**.

The process where one method passes values to another method, which then performs a task with that value, and returns a new value back to the calling method, can often be difficult to understand for new programmers. One way to help explain how it all works is to think of the sequence of events in the following real-world scenario:

> *Mr Maine's watch needs a new battery. He takes it to Mr Doblet, the jeweller on the High Street. The jeweller takes the watch into his workshop, and returns promptly with Mr Maine's watch, complete with a brand new battery fitted inside. Mr Maine thanks Mr Doblet, and goes home a satisfied customer.*

In this scenario, of course Mr Maine is playing the part of the **main** method, and Mr Doblet is playing the part of the **doubleIt** method. The watch is passed from Mr Maine to Mr Doblet, just like an input parameter is passed to a method that is called by another. Mr Doblet fixes the watch and returns it, updated with a new battery, to Mr Maine, just as the doubled value is returned to the **main** method in our program.

Mr Maine doesn't know how Mr Doblet changed the watch battery. He doesn't even care. Mr Doblet has provided a valuable service for Mr Maine, and he didn't mind waiting around while the job was being done. This is exactly how methods interact in Java.

As far as the **main** method is concerned, everything happens on the one line, where the **doubleIt** method is called. It doesn't *know* that **value** or **newValue** even exist, and it doesn't know how the double calculation is done (it could have been done like this: **newValue = value + value;**). The **doubleIt** method has provided a service for the **main** method, just as Mr Doblet did for Mr Maine.

In fact, you have already used methods that have been provided to you by other programmers many times already. All the following are methods that have been written by the developers of Java for other programmers to use in their own programs:

```
print("a string of text")
```

```
next()
```

```
nextInt()
```

```
nextDouble()
```

You have used these methods without knowing how they work or who wrote them. All you need to know is how they are to be called, and what data they require to operate correctly. These methods are providing a service for you.

Of course, you need to precede all of these methods with other words, such as **System. out**. Why you need to do this will be explained later when we look more closely at Java classes. For now, take it that the code which directly precedes the method call specifies the location where the method can be found in the Java environment (like an address in the real-world).

Hopefully, you can now see that writing methods is a very good idea, especially for large programs where several programmers may be working in a team. If one programmer writes a useful new method, it could be re-used by the whole team. That saves time and effort, and if the method is well-written and it works well, it will improve the reliability of programs that use it. The old adage: *why re-invent the wheel?* Certainly applies here!

Exercise 6.2: Circle area

 Design, build, and test a program that calculates the area of a circle, based on the user inputting its radius. You must write a separate method to calculate the formula: Area $= \pi r^2$

Working with several input parameters

So far, we have built methods that have no parameters, e.g. `clearScreen`, one input parameter, e.g. `outputSpaces`, and one input and one output parameter, e.g. `doubleIt`. We will now look at methods that use more than one input parameter.

Let's consider a simple example:

Design and build a program which works out the percentage of a number. Both the number and the percentage of that number required are input by the user. Write a separate method to perform the percentage calculation.

Here is the main design:

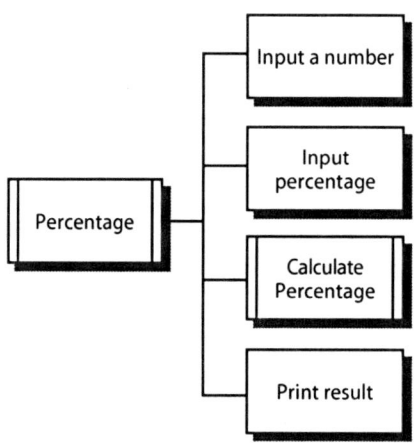

Here is the design of the **calculatePercentage** method:

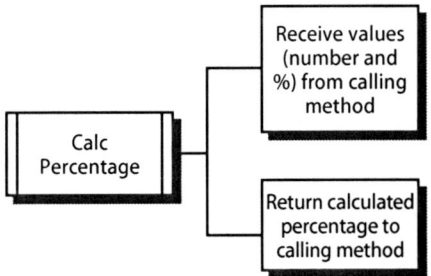

This is another relatively trivial problem to solve. We might not even choose to use a method if we were designing this problem. However, it makes sense to use a simple example when introducing a new technique or programming principle.

Rather than describe our Java program line by line, let's look at the whole thing and pick out the issues of interest:

```java
import java.util.Scanner;

/* Design and build a program which works out the percentage
   of a number. Both the number and the percentage of that
   number required are input by the user. */

class Percentage
{
    public static double calcPercentage(int num, double perc)
    {
        return (num * perc/100);
    }

    public static void main(String[] args)
    {
        Scanner input = new Scanner(System.in);

        int number;
        double percent;

        System.out.print("Input a number ");
        number = input.nextInt();

        System.out.print("Input a percentage ");
        percent = input.nextDouble();

        /* now call the calcPercentage method and output the
        result */
        System.out.print("The result is " +
                        calcPercentage(number, percent));
    }
}
```

Firstly, let's look at the **calcPercentage** method declaration:

```
public static double calcPercentage(int num, double perc)
```

We can see that we now have a method which is returning a **double** value to its calling method. We know this because the word **double** appears immediately after **public static**. We can also see that we now have two input parameters: **num** and **perc**. Notice how we declare them:

```
(int num, double perc)
```

> ### EXPERT GUIDANCE
>
> Here are some important things about input parameters:
>
> We have to specify explicitly the type of each parameter. If there are two **int** parameters, you have to specify each separately as a *type-variableName* pair.
>
> This is how to do it correctly for a three input parameter method
> **(int var1, int var2, double var3)** where the first two are integers, and the third is a double. This is how not to do it (a common mistake with new programmers): **(int var1, var2, double var3)**
>
> Notice that parameters are comma separated. Never use semi-colons in a parameter list.
>
> You can have as many input parameters as you like when you design your methods. What is crucial however, is that the order you pass them into the method (from the calling method) must be **EXACTLY** the same as the order in which they are received by the called method.

Let's consider our percentage calculator program again, and look at the line where the main method calls **calcPercentage**:

```
System.out.print("The result is " + calcPercentage(number,
percent));
```

Here, we have cleverly included the method call in the line where we print the result of the percentage calculation. What happens here is that when the Java program executes this line, just like in all lines of Java code, it executes what is inside the innermost round brackets first. So, the **calcPercentage** method is called, and the values of number and percent are sent to that method – **STRICTLY** in order. If we re-visit the **calcPercentage** method declaration, we'll see that the order of parameters declared match precisely that of the order of those that are sent to it:

```
public static double calcPercentage(int num, double perc)
```

So, the value of **number** is sent to **num**, and the value of **percent** is sent to **perc**. If we got these in the wrong order, the program would not work.

Once **calcPercentage** has executed, it returns a **double** value. We know this happens because we specified this in the method declaration. We should also know by now that double variables can be printed out on the console along with strings of text, integers and so forth. Therefore, there is no reason why we can't include *the double that is returned* from the **calcPercentage** method in the **System.out.print** line of code.

EXPERT GUIDANCE

The technique of including the method call in the print statement like this enables us to do more than one thing in a single line of code. Java allows extensive use of this practice. It is very popular with experienced programmers because very powerful and complex programs can be developed quickly and efficiently.

We've employed another clever technique in the **calcPercentage** method itself, where we do the percentage calculation AND return the result in the same line:

```
return (num * perc/100);
```

REMEMBER

What's in the brackets gets done first!

Exercise 6.3: Volume

 Add a new method to your circle area calculation program which calculates the volume of a cylinder with the same base area as the circle. Use the formula: Volume = area * height.

HINT: There are lots of ways to solve this problem, but the best way is to use the result returned from the area calculation method as an input to the calculate volume method!

Exercise 6.4: More pay

 Design, build and test a program to input the number of workers followed by their name, hours worked, hourly rate of pay, overtime rate of pay, status (married or single) for each. The main program must use separate methods and appropriate parameters. Suggested methods include:

- calculate the gross pay (overtime rate is paid for any number of hours above 40);

- calculate the amount of tax paid (25% if married and 30% if single);

- display all the details as a payslip on the computer screen.

HINT: You can pass String parameters too!

This is the end of the chapter on sub-programs. Once you have done the exercises above, you will have a reasonable understanding of how methods work. However, there is a lot more to methods than we have seen here. The following Java Forum may help to introduce some other concepts of methods, but if you want to further your knowledge significantly, you will need to consult a more advanced source.

Java Forum

Post	My method doesn't seem to do anything! Why? ⭐
Reply	A common mistake made by new programmers is to place a semi-colon at the end of a method declaration. For example:

```
public static double calcPercentage(int num, double
perc);
```

What happens here is that when the Java running program encounters the semi-colon, it thinks that the semi-colon means end-of-line, which as we know, it does. However, ending the line here means end-of-method too.

☺

Post	What are the parameters in the main method? ⭐
Reply	By now, you should understand most of what is happening in the **main** method declaration:

```
public static void main(String[] args)
```

The **void** term here means that the main method doesn't return a value. The **main** method cannot be called by other methods. However, it does accept input parameters, as is specified by the parameter list: **(String[] args)**.

This parameter list enables us to pass what we call **arguments** on the command line when we run the program. To illustrate this, here is a simple example program:

```
class Marriage
{
    public static void main(String[] args)
    {
        System.out.print(args[0] + " is married to " +
        args[1]);
    }
}
```

The first thing you might notice about this program is that there is no mention of the Scanner class – it isn't imported at the top of the program and we don't declare a Scanner object called **input**. In fact, it appears there is no input at all. However, we will be inputting from the command line, when we run the program. So, when the program has been compiled, we would run it like this:

```
java marriage Rich Liz
```

Rich and **Liz** are the two arguments we are sending to the marriage program. They are stored in a list of strings called **args**. The square brackets **[]** after the word **string** in the parameter list means that we can have many **args** passed to the main method. In this case, we have two, and we refer to them as **args[0]** (the first item) and **args[1]** (the second item) in the program. So, when the program runs, the following message will be output:

Rich is married to Liz

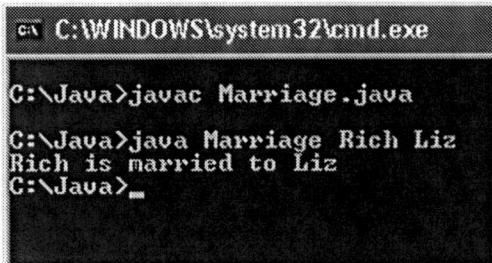

In Java, a list of items is called an **array**. Arrays are very powerful data structures which allow us to work with lists, or collections of data. We will develop our knowledge of arrays in the next chapter.

Chapter 7

ARRAYS

Chapter overview

So far in our programs, we have only worked with small numbers of variables and objects. Java provides us with several ways for us to manipulate large numbers of objects (e.g. transactions, records, stock items), which is something that most useful computer programs have to do. In this chapter, we will use a very powerful feature in Java called **arrays** to enable us to do this.

At the end of this chapter you will be able to:

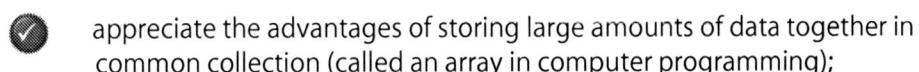 appreciate the advantages of storing large amounts of data together in a common collection (called an array in computer programming);

 design and write Java programs that use and manipulate collections of data.

Using arrays

You may remember that you have already encountered an **array** of objects, albeit very briefly, in the previous chapter. In the Java Forum, we looked at this program:

```
class Marriage
{
    public static void main(String[] args)
    {
        System.out.print(args[0] + " is married to " +
        args[1]);
    }
}
```

In the **main** method declaration, we passed an array of two **args** (arguments) from the command line. We referred to these as **args[0]** and **args[1]**. Each one contained a **String** object.

We can define our own arrays within programs in a similar way to how we declare other variables and objects. Here is a simple example, which enables the user to type in ten names and then prints the names in reverse order:

```
import java.util.Scanner;

/* Let the user type in 10 names, and print them in reverse
   order. */

class NameList
{

    public static void main(String[] args)
    {
        Scanner input = new Scanner(System.in);
        String[] name = new String[10];
        int count;

        for (count = 0; count < 10; count++)
        {
            System.out.print("Input a name ");
            name[count] = input.next();
        }

        for (count = 9; count >= 0; count--)
        {
            System.out.println(name[count]);
        }
    }
}
```

In the above program, we have declared and array called **name**. We have reserved 10 slots in the array to hold the 10 **String** objects we need to collect, like this:

```
String[] name = new String[10];
```

Each of the 10 objects is stored in an array that can be indexed, or referenced, by its position in the array. The first object in a Java array is at position 0, the next at position 1, and so on.

We use the **count** variable in our program to **index** each element of the array. We refer to each object in the array by placing its index in square brackets immediately after the array name, for example:

name[0] refers to the first object in the array

name[6] refers to the seventh object in the array

name[count] refers to the object stored at the index of whatever **count** is set to.

When our program runs, let's assume we type in the following names:

Alison, Bertie, Charlie, Dave, Eddie, Freda, Gertie, Harry, Ingrid, Joel.

In the computer's memory, each name is stored in the array at the following positions:

count	0	1	2	3	4	5	6	7	8	9
name	Alison	Bertie	Charlie	Dave	Eddie	Freda	Gertie	Harry	Ingrid	Joel

In the second loop in the program, we count down from 9 to 0 to output the names in reverse order. So, **name[9]** is printed first, then **name[8]**, and so on.

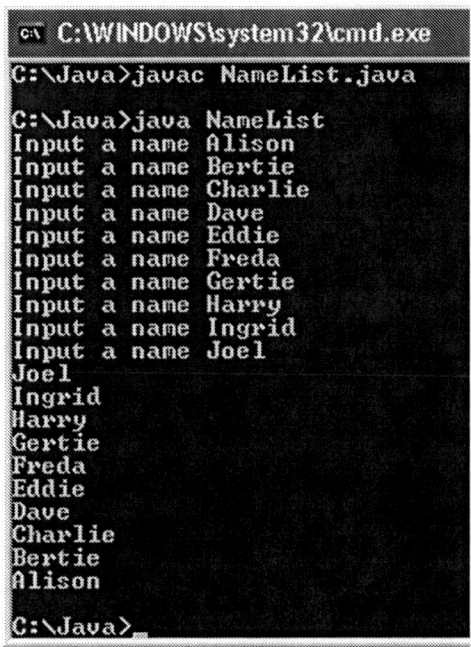

The example described works with arrays of **String** objects. We can work in the same way with other variables, such as **int** and **double**.

Exercise 7.1: Ice skaters

 Design and build a program to enable a user to input an array of six integers, which represent the scores allocated by judges in an ice skating competition. Once all scores have been entered into the array, use it to calculate and output the average score.

 Modify your program to omit the lowest and highest score allocated, taking the middle four marks as the basis on which to calculate the average.

Working with groups of information

Arrays enable us to group together related information, and to perform actions on the group as a whole, or on individual elements of the group. We have already carried out both these types of operations. For example, we took a list of names and printed it out in reverse order. The group of information in this case, of course, was the *list*. In the last exercise, you also manipulated a group of information (the *set* of scores), and then you performed actions on individual elements in the set of scores to omit the highest and lowest marks.

> **NOTE**
>
> Typical operations that computer programs perform on groups of information (e.g. lists, sets, tables, records, transactions, charts – the list is endless) include:
>
> - *finding* specific things, e.g. the highest earner amongst a group of workers;
> - *summarising* the group, e.g. calculating the average daily temperature over a month;
> - *sorting* things into some kind of order, e.g. an alphabetical list of students in a computer class;
> - *manipulating* the group, e.g. moving an army of space invaders across a screen in a computer game.

The ice-skating exercises enabled you to perform finding and summarising. We will now look at a way we can use arrays to help us sort information.

We will begin our look at **sorting** by introducing the simplest type of sort possible – we will sort a list of just two items. If we need to sort the items, we effectively swap them around. Whilst swapping may seem a trivial task, it does cause us a slight problem. Let's look at a real-world example to help explain the issue here. Consider this:

> *Fred buys two pints of beer at his local pub, a real ale for himself and a lager for his friend Jim. Fred and Jim have been loyal customers for years and have their own tankards behind the bar, which the landlord always uses for their drinks. However, today there is a new barman on duty. He has heard about the trusty tankards, but he gets the lager and the real ale mixed up. Fred's tankard is full of lager and Jim's contains the real ale. The barman offers to pour the drinks down the sink and start again, but the thrifty Fred insists that it'll be fine to swap the contents around. How does he do this?*

The answer is obvious, of course. The barman pours off one tankard into a spare glass, then pours the other tankard into the now empty tankard, and finally he takes the spare glass and pours that into the most recently emptied tankard. There are three steps to this operation. We can express what the barman has done slightly more formally, like this:

1. contents of spare glass = contents of tankard A
2. contents of tankard A = contents of tankard B
3. contents of tankard B = contents of spare glass

The point here is that we needed an extra glass to do the simple swap. We couldn't just swap the items around because the containers (the glasses in this case) couldn't hold the two pints at once. In Java, these containers would be variables, or perhaps array elements. We know in Java that a variable can't hold two values at once, so in effect, the example of the two pints of liquid is a good one, because we need to perform the same sequence of three steps to swap two variables.

Let's now look at how we might express a simple **swap** in a Java program. We will swap the values of two variables, **x** and **y**.

```
/* Swap two items */

class SwapIt
{

   public static void main(String[] args)
   {
       int x = 10;
       int y = 20;
       int temp;

       temp = x;
       x = y;
       y = temp;

       System.out.println(x);
       System.out.println(y);
   }
}
```

Now we will do the same thing, but this time we will use an array, called **numList**. We will then discuss the program, as there are some new Java statements to consider.

```
/* Swap two items */

class SwapItAgain
{

   public static void main(String[] args)
   {
       int[] numList = {10,20};
       int temp;

       temp = numList[0];
       numList[0] = numList[1];
       numList[1] = temp;

       System.out.println(numList[0]);
       System.out.println(numList[1]);
   }
}
```

The first thing you might notice about both programs is that there is no use of the Scanner class. Like the **Marriage** program (*see page 108*), there is no input by the user at all, so we don't actually need to import the Scanner class. Both programs use the same method (or **algorithm**, to introduce another term used in computer programming). They perform the swap with a variable called **temp**, which acts as a temporary container for one of the values.

The second program, **SwapItAgain**, uses an integer array called **numList** to hold the two values.

EXPERT GUIDANCE

Notice how numList is declared:

```
int[] numList = {10,20};
```

The declaration of the array also contains initial values of 10 and 20 for the two integer slots (separated by commas, and listed in curly brackets). This is a very neat feature of Java array declaration, where several values can be initialised in a quick and easy way. Here is a more verbose version which produces exactly the same outcome:

```
int[] numList = new int[2];

numList[0] = 10;

numList[1] = 20;
```

Notice how similar the integer array declaration above is to the way we declared the String array in the **NameList** program.

```
String[] name = new String[10];
```

Exercise 7.2: Initialise a list

 Modify the **NameList** program so that no user input is required to enter the list of names. Instead of the user entering ten names, initialise a new list of names in the String declaration statement.

Now that we know how to swap two values in a program, we can apply the same principle to performing a more complex sort of many items. There are many ways we can sort things in the real world – imagine the number of techniques you could use to sort a pack of cards for example. There are many different kinds of sorting algorithms widely used by computer programmers. We will look at the simplest. It's called a **bubble sort**. It is given this name because items **bubble** up and down the unsorted list like liquid bubbles might do in a test tube when experiencing a chemical reaction.

Our program will sort a list of ten numbers into ascending order. In the program, we will swap any values next to each other in the list where the first value is larger than its neighbour. We keep on doing this again and again until there are no more swaps to do. We will look at the bubble sort technique with an example before we actually write the program. Here is a list of numbers from 1 to 10 grouped arbitrarily:

```
7,10,3,1,2,5,9,4,6,8
```

Here is the same group of numbers, this time indexed from 0 to 9:

count	0	1	2	3	4	5	6	7	8	9
number	7	10	3	1	2	5	9	4	6	8

The bubble sort would work on this list of numbers to sort them in ascending order as follows:

- Take the first number (7) and compare it with the second (10). Is the first one greater than the second?
- The answer is no, so we do nothing – they are already in order.
- Now take the second number (10) and compare it with the next number (3). Is it greater than the next number?
- The answer is yes, so we swap them around, giving us the modified list:

count	0	**1**	**2**	3	4	5	6	7	8	9
number	7	**3**	**10**	1	2	5	9	4	6	8

- Now take the next pair of numbers, which are 10 and 1. Is the first one greater than the second?
- The answer is yes, so we swap them around, giving us another modified list:

count	0	1	**2**	**3**	4	5	6	7	8	9
number	7	3	**1**	**10**	2	5	9	4	6	8

- Now take the next pair of numbers, which are 10 and 2. Is the first one greater than the second?
- The answer is yes, so we swap them around, giving us yet another modified list:

count	0	1	2	**3**	**4**	5	6	7	8	9
number	7	3	1	**2**	**10**	5	9	4	6	8

- By now, you should be able to see that the largest number in the list (10) is gradually bubbling its way to the end of the list.
- Once all pairs of numbers have been compared, we have this in our list:

count	0	1	2	3	4	5	6	7	8	9
number	7	3	1	2	5	9	4	6	8	10

- Now the number 10 is in its rightful position. However, there is still more work to do to get the numbers fully sorted.
- Basically, we start from the beginning of the list again, and keep comparing the pairs of numbers. So next, we compare the number 7 with the number 3.
- Of course, we will swap the numbers to give:

count	0	1	2	3	4	5	6	7	8	9
number	3	7	1	2	5	9	4	6	8	10

- The number 7 will continue to bubble through the list until it hits the number 9:

count	0	1	2	3	4	5	6	7	8	9
number	3	1	2	5	7	9	4	6	8	10

- At this point, the number 9 takes precedence, and the number 7 remains in its place for now. However, now the 9 and the 4 must swap when they are compared.
- Following this the 9 and 6, then the 9 and 8 must also swap places. When we have gone through the whole list for the second time, we have the following:

count	0	1	2	3	4	5	6	7	8	9
number	3	1	2	5	7	4	6	8	9	10

It is rapidly becoming clear that the list is now beginning to take some sort of order. With a few more runs through our bubble sort method, the list will soon be sorted.

The design for the bubble sort algorithm naturally uses loops. Whilst stepping through the way it works, hopefully this was apparent. In fact, the bubble sort involves a **while** loop *and* a **for** loop.

The **while** loop is there to enable the list to be examined over and over again until no more sorting is required. We don't know how many times the loop will need to run, because it will vary with different sets of numbers. The more sorted the list is initially, the fewer passes through the loop will be required.

We will use a **boolean** variable called **sorted** to control the loop. A **boolean** variable can have one of two values, simply **true** or **false**. These are both keywords in Java, so make sure you never declare variables with these names.

Initially, we will set the value of the variable to **false**. When the list is fully sorted, we will set its value to **true**. In the program, the **while** statement will look like this:

```
while (! sorted)
```

which can be read as *while not sorted*. This is just the same as:

```
while (sorted == false)
```

and:

```
while (sorted != true)
```

All are acceptable in Java.

The **for** loop is there to enable the pairs of numbers to be compared through the list. We always know that this must be done a given number of times. For a list of ten numbers, we will need nine comparisons: the 1st with the 2nd, the 2nd with the 3rd, the 3rd with the 4th, the 4th with the 5th, the 5th with the 6th, the 6th with the 7th, the 7th with the 8th, the 8th with the 9th, and the 9th with the 10th. In fact, the number of comparisons is always one less than the length of the list.

The design for the program looks like this:

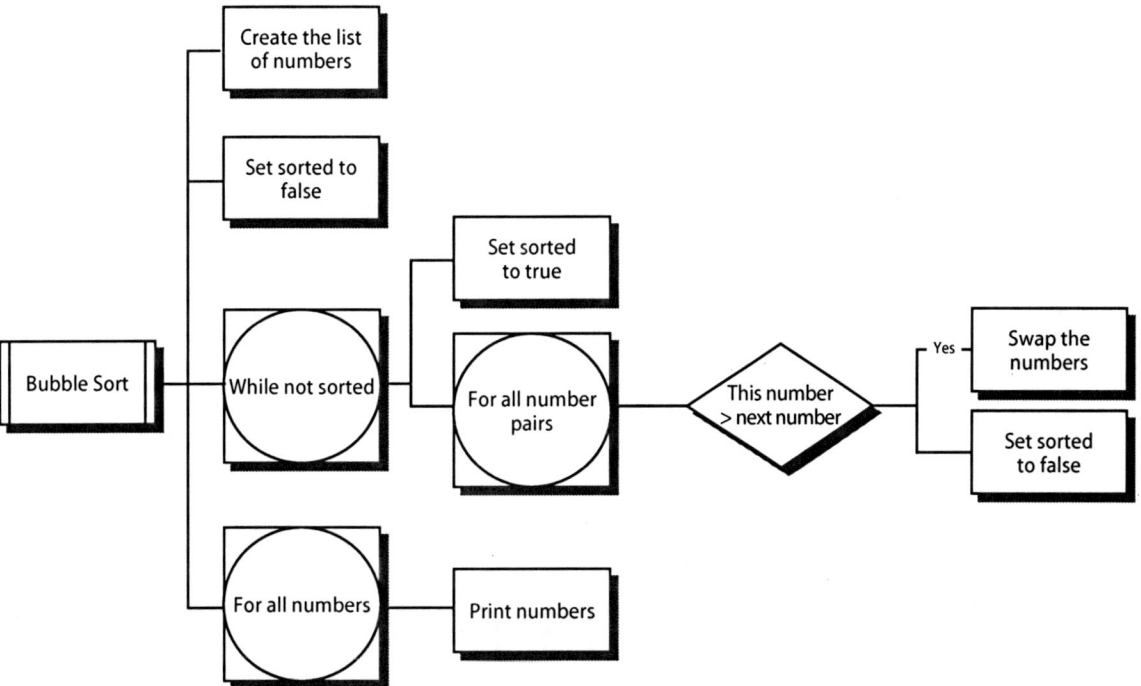

The Java code looks like this:

```java
/* Perform a bubble sort on a list of 10 integers */

class Sort
{

    public static void main(String[] args)
    {
        int[] numList = {7,10,3,1,2,5,9,4,6,8};
        int temp, count;
        boolean sorted = false;

        while (!sorted)
        {
            // assume list is sorted until proven otherwise
            sorted = true;

            for (count = 0; count <= 8; count++) /* loop 9
            times */
            {
                /* compare a number with its immediate
                neighbour */
                if (numList[count] > numList[count+1])
                {
                    // swap the two numbers
                    temp = numList[count];
                    numList[count] = numList[count+1];
                    numList[count+1] = temp;

                    // reset control as still sorting to do!
                    sorted = false;
                }
            }
        }

        // print out the sorted list
        for (count = 0; count <= 9; count++)
            System.out.println(numList[count]);
    }
}
```

NOTE

Notice how we have cleverly used the count variable to index pairs of numbers, by adding one to count whenever we want to examine a number with its immediate neighbour:

```java
numList[count] // refers to this number
numList[count+1] // refers to next number
```

Exercise 7.3: Saver bonus

In this exercise you will show how you can use arrays to manipulate grouped information. Every Christmas, the Famously Good Building Society awards a bonus to all its savers, expressed as a percentage of the balance of each account. Design, code and test a program to enable a user to type in four savers' balances and the percentage bonus (which is the same for everyone). The program should then output the new balances for each saver.

Using arrays with methods

In the last chapter, we looked at how we can use Java methods to improve our programming practice. As we have seen, methods have many advantages:

- they help us to avoid duplicating code;
- they make programs easier to read;
- they make programs easier to change or modify;
- they make programs more reliable;
- they make programs easier to design;
- they allow many people to work on the same program or system.

Java supports the use of methods and arrays together. Arrays can be used as both input and output parameters, enabling us to process groups of information with all the advantages that methods provide us. As an example, we will convert the bubble sorting program to one that uses methods.

Firstly, we'll start with the design. Using stepwise refinement makes the design easier to read. Here is the main method:

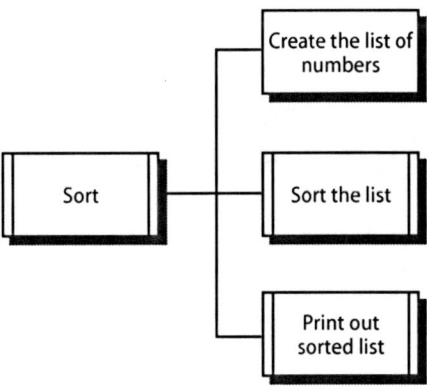

We have two new methods. One performs the sort, and the other prints it. The sort method is designed like this:

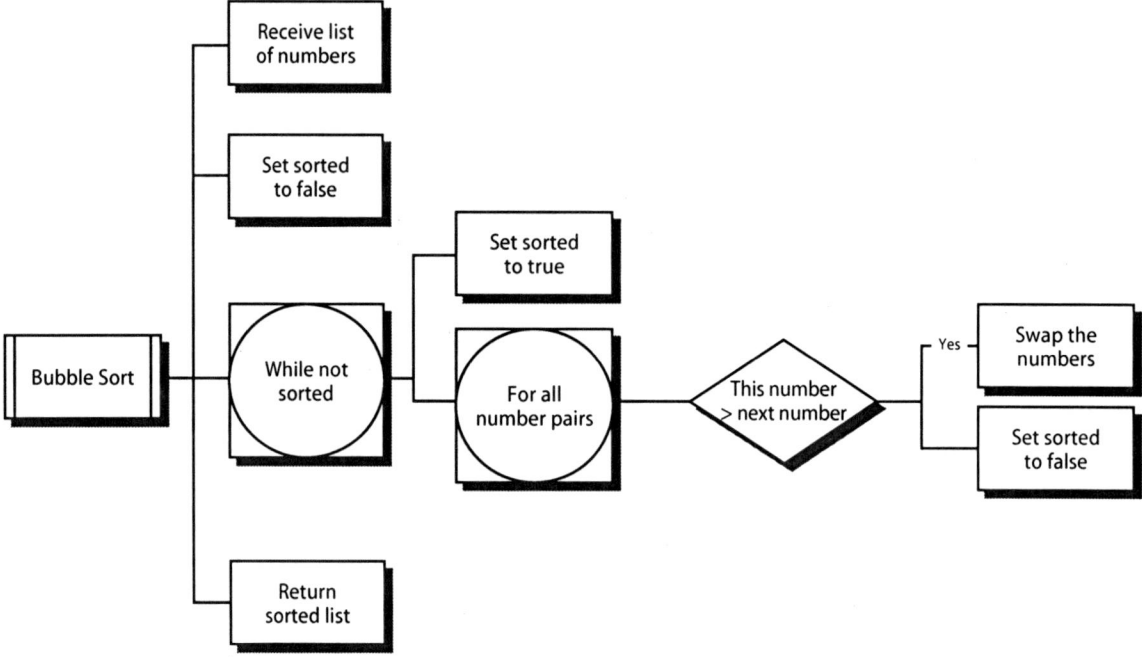

Here is the printing method:

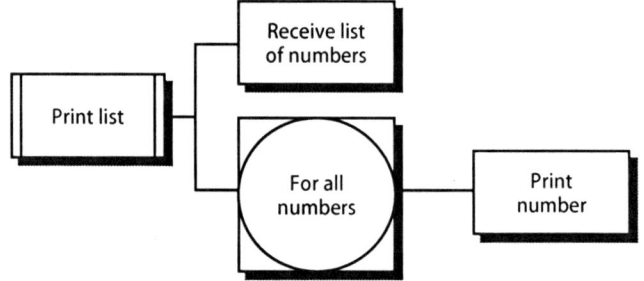

Finally, the program itself. See if you can spot some new Java in the program.

```
/* Perform a bubble sort on a list of 10 integers */

class Sorted
{

    public static int[] bubbleSort(int[] list)
    {
        int temp, count;
        boolean sorted = false;

        while (sorted == false)
        {
            sorted = true;

            for (count = 0; count <= (list.length - 2);
            count++)
            {
                if (list[count] > list[count+1])
                {
                    // swap the two numbers
                    temp = list[count];
                    list[count] = list[count+1];
                    list[count+1] = temp;
                    sorted = false; // still sorting to do!
                }
            }
        }

        return list;
    }

    public static void printList(int[] sortedList)
    {
        for (int count = 0;
            count <= (sortedList.length - 1); count++)
            System.out.println(sortedList[count]);
    }

    public static void main(String[] args)
    {
        int[] numList = {7,10,3,1,2,5,9,4,6,8};

        numList = bubbleSort(numList);

        printList(numList);
    }
}
```

Notice how small the main method is. It reflects exactly the simplicity of its design. In the new bubble sorting method, you should be able to see how we pass array parameters in Java. It's a similar technique as with more simple data types, but we need to include the square brackets `[]` in the parameter list (just as you've always done with the `main` method).

In both the **bubbleSort** method and the **printList** method, we have used some new Java. Rather than having to remember the size (or length) of the array we are working with, we can use a Java feature called **length** which will give us the size of the array without us having to remember it ourselves. In our program, the size is 10, so we perform a simple bit of subtraction to give us the desired condition to end the **for** loops:

```
for (count = 0; count <= (list.length - 2); count++) /* count
from 0-8 */

for (int count = 0;
    count <= (sortedList.length - 1); count++) /* count from
    0-9 */
```

The beauty of what we have done in our new program is not just that it uses methods, but that the methods we have written are coded in such a way that they will work with any size of array. Our array could be 100 numbers long, but the methods will still work because we've used the **length** feature. We now have generic methods which we could use in *any* other program that needs to print a list, or sort a list of numbers. Hopefully you can see how methods are very powerful in supporting the *re-use* of code.

Exercise 7.4: Savers with methods

 Modify the Famously Good Building Society program to use methods. Use separate methods for the following functions:

 enable a user to type in four savers' balances;

 update the balances by applying the percentage bonus;

output the new balances for each saver.

Arrays provide very powerful ways to enable programmers to manipulate and structure data. We have only scratched the surface in terms of the opportunities and applications of arrays. There are also many other ways of dealing with grouped information in Java. In the next chapter we will use arrays further, to manipulate more complex data structures. However, the full range of possibilities is beyond the scope of this book.

Java Forum

Post	Why does indexing start at zero and not one? ⭐
Reply	The answer to this question is that it just does! Some programming languages begin array indexing at one, but not Java! Make sure you remember that the first element of an array is at index zero. If you try to access array elements outside the allocated space you set when you declare the array, you may find that your program will crash, so be careful! ☺
Post	**I keep getting an error which says my array isn't initialised, but I have declared it in my main method!** ⭐
Reply	In Java, you **MUST** initialise an array before you use it. You can do this in two ways. Firstly, by populating it with values. For example:

```
int[] numList = {7,10,3,1,2,5,9,4,6,8};
```

Secondly, if you don't want to give your array values, you can initialise it like this:

```
int[] numList = new int[10];
```

☺

Post	**My array is huge and I want to set all the initial values to 0. How do I do this without having to type a VERY long line?** ⭐
Reply	It would of course be a tedious, not to mention difficult, task to use the first initialisation technique (above) to do this. In Java, the best way would be to use the second technique, followed by a **for** loop to populate the array. For example:

```
int[] myArray = new int[100];
for (int count = 0; count <= (myArray.length - 1);
count++)
    myArray [count] = 0;
```

☺

Chapter 8

CLASSES

Chapter overview

In this final chapter, we will see that we can develop programs with several Java classes, thereby giving us even more power and flexibility in our programs. Classes provide us with advanced ways to design and organise our programs, and enable us to develop well-engineered solutions.

At the end of this chapter you will be able to:

- ✓ appreciate the nature of Java as an *object-oriented* language;

- ✓ design and write programs that use several classes and objects;

- ✓ understand the rudiments of object-oriented programming;

- ✓ decide where you want to go from here – perhaps move on to develop bigger, more exciting programs!

Classes you have used already

Just as you were using several Java methods developed by other programmers (e.g. **print**, **nextInt**) before you wrote your own earlier, you have already used other classes in your programs which were written by the people who developed Java. You might have worked this out already: the classes you have used are **Scanner**, **System** and **String**. A big clue here is that Java classes tend to begin their names in upper case.

Objects

When we use a class, we can construct **objects** which behave in the way defined by that class. You have already constructed objects in Java in virtually every program you have written:

```
Scanner input = new Scanner(System.in);
```

This line of code constructs a new **Scanner object**, which we have called input. The parameter **System.in** tells the new object to scan input from the keyboard.

The **Scanner class** has been written by the developers of Java. The diagram on the following page shows a simplified representation of the class:

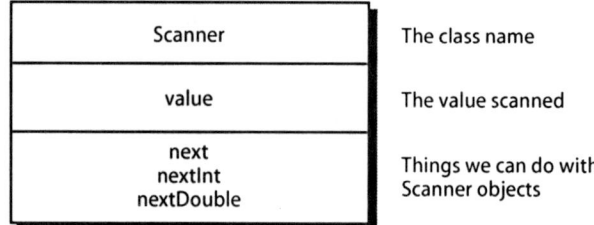

The *things we can do with Scanner objects* are, of course, all Java methods. When we have created an object, we can then call the methods that are associated with that object. In all our programs, we named the Scanner object **input**. We use a **dot** (.) in between the object name and the method whenever we call it:

```
input.next();
```

```
input.nextInt();
```

```
input.nextDouble();
```

Calling a method in another class is termed *sending a message* to that class. There are many other methods that Scanner objects understand, but we will not deal with them here. If you are interested, you can browse the Java class libraries at **http://java.sun.com** where you will find thousands of pages of information. Just looking at this website will give you an idea about just how big and how powerful Java really is. Java relies very heavily on classes and their objects. This is why Java is called an **object-oriented** language.

Writing classes in Java

We have already written single class programs in Java. All our programs contain at least one class, of course. Here, we will write a program with two simple classes. Here is the problem specification for the program:

> Design and write a program which enables a user to add two books to a collection. The books have a title and a date of publication. Once the two books have been added, a message should be output which lists the most recently published book.

Here is the design for the program:

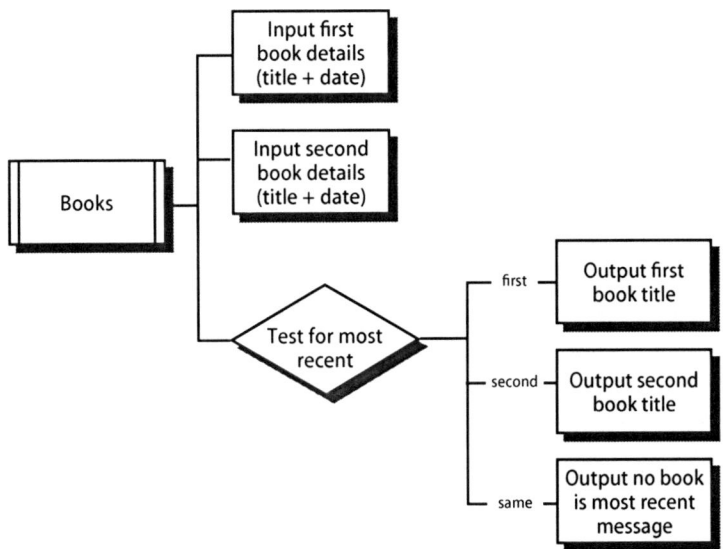

We could write a program to solve this problem using the techniques we already know. In fact, we could write ANY computer program using the techniques we already know. However, classes extend our toolset, and enable us to build better solutions. Of course, the same principles apply to all forms of building or engineering. You could always build a house with no more than wood, a hammer and some nails, but it wouldn't last, and it wouldn't be as good as one built with bricks and mortar.

DESIGN GUIDELINE

Design guideline: designing with classes

To design a program that uses classes, we need to identify the objects in the problem specification that can be described in terms of the things we can do with them (their *methods*), and the things that uniquely identify them (their **attributes**). In our example here, we will create a class called **Book**. The methods will be called **Book** (simply to add a book to the library), **getTitle** and **getDate** (to get information about a book once it's in the library). The attributes will be a book's title, and its publication date. The **Book** class can be described in the following diagram:

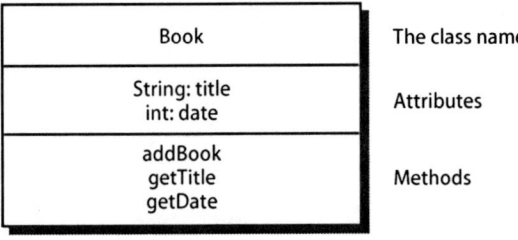

We can write the **Book** class in Java like this:

```
/* The Book class */
class Book
{
    private String title;
    private int date;

    Book (String t, int d)
    {
        title = t;
        date = d;
    }

    String getTitle()
    {
        return title;
    }


    int getDate()
    {
        return date;
    }
}
```

In the **Book** class, we have our attributes declared at the top: **title** and **date**. Notice how we use the Java keyword **private** in the declaration. This keyword means that we don't want any other class in the program to manipulate the attributes directly. Rather, we would prefer to give the **Book** class full authority in controlling them. This is good programming practice, as it would be dangerous to allow free manipulation of attributes elsewhere in the program. The **Book** class has a job to do, and that is to keep information about books. This principle applies in the real world, where people take responsibility for certain artefacts in their jobs. For example, a librarian would not allow their date stamper to be used by a customer. A payroll officer would not allow employees to enter their own monthly salary. In Java, the practice of keeping access to attributes and methods private to particular classes is called **data encapsulation**.

The methods are declared below. They are not private to the class, and can therefore be called by other classes, in this case the class that contains the **main** method, which is shown here:

```
class Library
{

    public static void main(String[] args)
    {
        Scanner input = new Scanner(System.in);
        String bookTitle;
        int pubDate;

        System.out.print
            ("Enter the title and date for the first book ");
        bookTitle = input.next();
        pubDate = input.nextInt();

        Book book1 = new Book(bookTitle,pubDate);

        System.out.print
            ("Enter the title and date for the second book ");
        bookTitle = input.next();
        pubDate = input.nextInt();

        Book book2 = new Book(bookTitle,pubDate);

        if (book1.getDate() > book2.getDate())
            System.out.print(book1.getTitle());
        else if (book2.getDate() > book1.getDate())
            System.out.print(book2.getTitle());
        else System.out.print("Neither");

        System.out.print(" is the most recent book!");

    }

}
```

We will step through the **Library** class now, and describe how the **Book** class is used.

The first thing to point out here is that the original design we produced for the program matches the logic of the **Library** class perfectly. We input the book details, test them, and output a message telling us the most recent book.

What's new here is that we are creating book **objects** whenever we enter a new book into the system. Once we have created a book object, we can retrieve its details later. Objects are stored in the computer's memory, just like variables, but they are more powerful and we have more control over them. Our book object has two attributes, for example, which are a **String** (which itself we know to be an object in Java), and an **int** variable, for the date.

In the **Library** class, we enter the first book's details with the following code:

```
System.out.print("Enter the title and date for the first book ");
bookTitle = input.next();
pubDate = input.nextInt();
```

This technique follows exactly the same approach as we have used in previous chapters. The next line creates a book object, called **book1**:

```
Book book1 = new Book(bookTitle, pubDate);
```

The format of this line is very similar to a line which features in virtually all your Java programs, where you create a **Scanner** object to enable you to input data from your keyboard:

```
Scanner input = new Scanner(System.in);
```

When we create an object, we firstly write the name of the class of object we wish to create. In the library program, we want to create a **Book** object. Next, we give the object a name. We have called ours **book1**. Next, we use the keyword **new** to indicate that we are introducing a brand new object. Finally, we call the method in the **Book** class which adds the book to the library (which we've called **Book**), including the attributes of the book, which we pass as parameters. In this case, **bookTitle** and **pubDate**.

EXPERT GUIDANCE

The method that creates the new object is known as a **constructor**. It is sensible to use the same name for a constructor as that of the class where it belongs. In this case, the class and constructor method are both called **Book**.

We can produce as many objects as we like. In the example, we create another book called **book2**.

Next, we can retrieve the book objects and use them in our program. We do this by calling the methods in the **Book** class, making sure we specify exactly which object we want to use. We do this by prefixing the object's name (followed by a **dot**), as in this example, which gets the title of **book1** and prints it on the screen:

```
System.out.print(book1.getTitle());
```

We can use objects' methods just like any other Java method. This line from the program compares the publication dates of the two books:

```
if (book1.getDate() > book2.getDate())
```

Exercise 8.1: Author

 Add a new attribute to the Book class called author. In your main method, after comparing dates, write another test to establish if the author of the two books is the same person.

More on classes

We have just seen that by using classes, we can structure our programs in a way which enables us to think about the **objects** we are working with. This is useful in itself to help us break down a program into smaller, more manageable components. It enables us to think about not just the attributes of objects, but also the things we allow ourselves to do with those objects (the object's methods).

Another very useful feature of classes is that we can organise them in a very efficient and well-structured way. Simply speaking, we can create classifications for our classes. People who organise information do this all the time – shop owners classify their goods, television producers classify programmes, hospitals classify patients, employees, operations, uniforms, etc. In fact, pretty much any situation where there is a lot of information involves the classification of that information – just so it can more easily be managed. This classification usually involves some kind of hierarchy, where classes are described in more detail by defining what we might call groups of sub-classes. The diagram below shows a simple example of this idea:

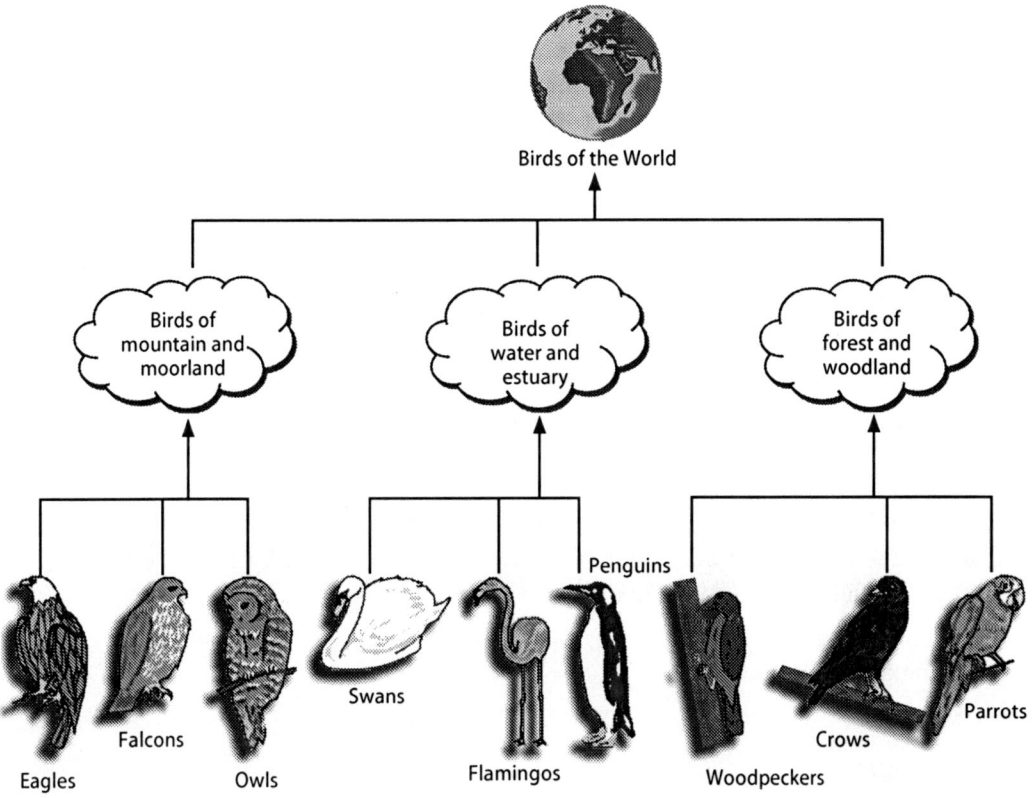

Here, we have a diagram showing birds of the world[1], which have been classified according to their habitat. They are then classified by their breed. So, we could say that a sub-class of the *super* class *Birds of the World* is *Birds of mountain and moorland*, and a sub-class of this is *Eagles*.

---

1 Apologies to all ornithologists for the over-simplification of this bird classification!

By classifying our information in this way, we can identify things that are common at each level of the hierarchy. At the top level, we know that all birds have wings, feathers, two legs and two eyes. The birds of mountain and moorland all fly, but the birds of water and estuary don't all fly (penguins can't!). Wings, feathers, etc. are clearly **attributes** of the birds, and fly, swim, eat mice are all clearly *things that birds do*, which we would envisage as **methods** in a Java program.

In terms of the hierarchy, it is also clear that, for example, an eagle *is a* bird of mountain and moorland, which *is a* bird of the World. So, if all birds have feathers, wings, two eyes and two legs, and all birds of mountain and moorland have forward-facing eyes, talons, eat mice and soar, we can safely say that all eagles have all of those attributes and do all of these things. This characteristic, where sub-classes take on the properties of their super-classes, is called inheritance. Inheritance is an important feature of the Java programming language, so we will continue to talk about it in the next section.

Inheritance

We write computer programs more often than not which handle large amounts of information. It makes sense therefore to provide specific ways to help programmers and program designers to classify that information. Of course, we can use classes to do this for us. Inheritance is a characteristic of classes which enable us to develop reliable, efficient, and powerful programs. We will illustrate inheritance in Java with another example from the real world, and will re-visit the Book exercise to introduce the new Java code:

Consider a lending library full of books, magazines, reference dictionaries, encyclopaedias, maybe also videos and CD-ROMs. All of these reading materials (library media) have things in common, perhaps they are catalogued in a similar way: they all have a title, a subject type, a date of publication and so forth. However, there are some things that are specific to different media. Books have ISBNs, whereas CD-ROMs and videos don't; books can be borrowed by users of the library, whereas reference dictionaries can't.

Librarians are specialists in *classifying* the books, magazines and other media they administer. If we wanted to write a computer program to help the librarians in our scenario to do this, we could start by classifying the reading materials so that we can describe both the similarities and differences between them. This would be a good idea because if, for example, we wanted to borrow a book from the library, we could easily know from the book's classification whether it could actually be borrowed or not.

Let's begin by considering the things that are common to all library media. We can divide these things into two categories:

● their description; and

● the things we can do with them.

We will use the diagramming technique from earlier to describe this information, as shown on the following page:

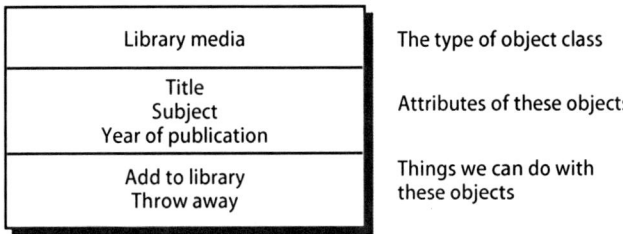

The diagram is divided into three sections:

Library media is the title of the things (or objects) we are dealing with. We can refer to this as the *class* of object. In fact, we'll just call this diagram *Library media class*.

Title, Subject and *Year of publication* are descriptions (or attributes) of the things common to library media.

Add to library and *Throw away* are things we can do to any library media. When the librarian buys a book, it can be added to the library stock. When it is no longer of any use, it can be disposed of. These will be our Java methods for library media.

Let's now consider a similar diagram, this time specifically for books:

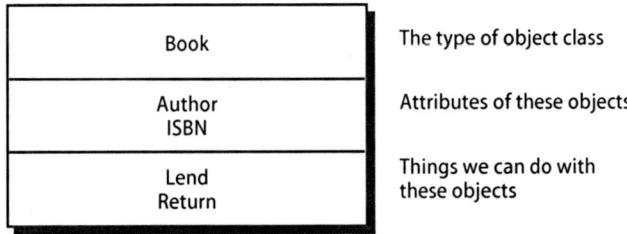

Again, the diagram is divided into three sections. We will call it *Book class*. You may notice that there is not a title, subject, year of publication, or anything else in here that was previously described in the Library media class. The reason for this is that, as you've probably realised by now, we really don't like duplication in programming or program design. Instead, we can combine the two class diagrams, like this:

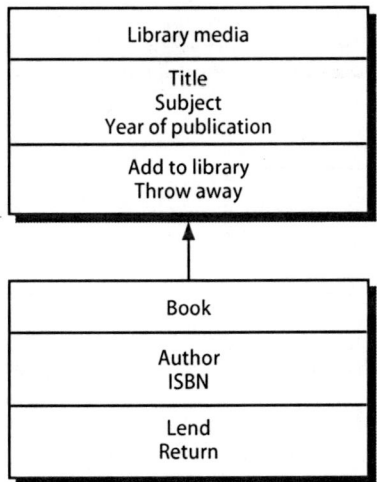

The way we read this diagram is to say that the Book class also has the properties of the Library media class. The Book class **inherits** from the Library media class. So, the complete set of attributes for the book class is a combination of the Book and Library media class:

- Title
- Subject
- Year of publication
- Author
- ISBN

The things we can do with a book are:

- Add to library
- Throw away
- Lend
- Return

Similarly, we could describe another class of object, this time a video:

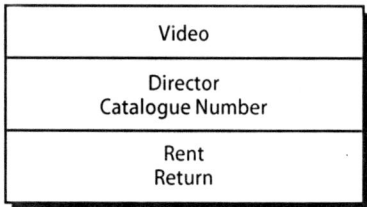

We can combine the three classes like this:

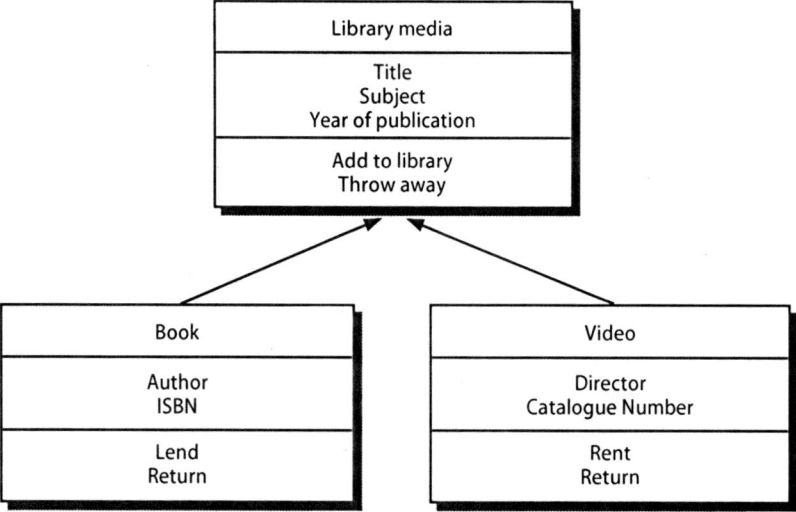

We could go on to describe the whole library in a similar way, but that would be a long and complicated process. Instead we will assume that the library only stocks books and videos.

So, we have three classes:

- Library media

- Book

- Video

For the purposes of this exercise, we won't worry about how the library system works here. All we are concerned about is how the classes interact in terms of their inheritance characteristics. We will do this by looking at the class definitions in Java, firstly by looking at the Library media class:

```java
/* The Library media class */
class LibraryMedia
{
    private String title;
    private String subject;
    private int date;

    LibraryMedia (String t, String s, int d)
    {
        title = t;
        subject = s;
        date = d;
    }

    String getTitle()
    {
        return title;
    }

    String getSubject()
    {
        return subject;
    }

    int getDate()
    {
        return date;
    }
}
```

If you compare this to the **Book** class from our earlier example, you'll see that the two are very similar. We have the attributes defined at the top of the class and the method definitions below.

Our new book class looks like this:

```
/* The Book class */
class Book extends LibraryMedia
{
    private String author;
    private int isbn;

    Book (String t, String s, int d , String a, int i)
    {
        super (t, s, d); // super class constructor

        author = a;
        isbn = i;
    }

    String getAuthor()
    {
        return author;
    }

    int getIsbn()
    {
        return isbn;
    }
}
```

NOTE

There are some new Java terms in the **Book** class. The class definition itself reads:

```
class Book extends LibraryMedia
```

The new Java keyword **extends** states that **Book** is a sub-class of **LibraryMedia**. It therefore inherits its super-class properties. This means that a book object also possesses the attributes of the **LibraryMedia** class, as well as its methods.

When we create a book object by calling the **Book** constructor, we must also create a **LibraryMedia** object by including the following line in the **Book** constructor method:

```
super (t, s, d); // super class constructor
```

The new keyword **super** calls the constructor of the object's super class.

Exercise 8.2: Music

Draw a class diagram which describes what you know about three musical instruments. The instruments are piano, guitar, and violin. All of them have strings and all of them make a sound. Pianos have keys and violins have bows. You can strum a guitar and a violin, but you can't strum a piano – you have to hit the keys. Show some other properties and actions that can be performed with the instruments. To structure your class model, use a super class, called **`Instrument`**.

Exercise 8.3: Museum

Draw a class diagram and write the Java code to represent a vehicle museum. Vehicles have a licence plate, a year of manufacture, a value, and a colour. The museum has cars, which have a number of doors, seats, engine type (petrol or diesel), and engine size in litres. The museum also has motorbikes, which have a bike type (sports, tourer, or trails), and engine size in cubic centimetres (cc). Note that you are not expected to run the program – all you need to do is show how the class structures can be coded in Java.

Working with classes, objects, methods and arrays

We have now seen and worked with all of the features of Java required to complete this introductory text. We will now put everything together by developing a much larger program than those we have previously designed and built. In this program, we will revisit many techniques and ideas already covered in previous chapters. The purpose of this is to reinforce your knowledge of program design, Java, and of computer programming in general.

We will use the Library program as the basis for this, which was introduced at the beginning of this chapter. In this program, we created two new books and compared their dates. We will now develop further this program so it can deal with many book objects.

Here is the specification for the new program:

> **Design and write a program which enables a user to manage books in a library. The user will be presented with the following options in a menu when the program runs. The options available are:**
>
> 1. add a book to the collection. All books have a title, an author and a date of publication;
>
> 2. list all books written by a particular author;
>
> 3. list all books published in a given year;
>
> 0. quit the program.

For this problem, we have added a new attribute to the **Book** class: the book's author. We will also need a new method to retrieve the author of a book, which we will call **getAuthor**. The class diagram therefore now looks like this:

The new **Book** class looks like this in Java:

```java
/* The Book class */
class Book
{
    private String title;
    private String author;
    private int date;

    Book (String t, String a, int d)
    {
        title = t;
        author = a;
        date = d;
    }

    String getTitle()
    {
        return title;
    }

    String getAuthor()
    {
        return author;
    }

    int getDate()
    {
        return date;
    }
}
```

Now we will design the methods. Obviously we need a **main** method. Additionally, we will design methods to perform the following jobs:

- display a menu of choices to the user and enable the user to select their chosen option;
- add a book to the collection;

- list all books written by a particular author;
- list all books published in a given year.

We will start with the **main** method. This method will be responsible purely for calling the other methods, depending on the user's selection. There is a loop in this method which will cycle until the user quits the program:

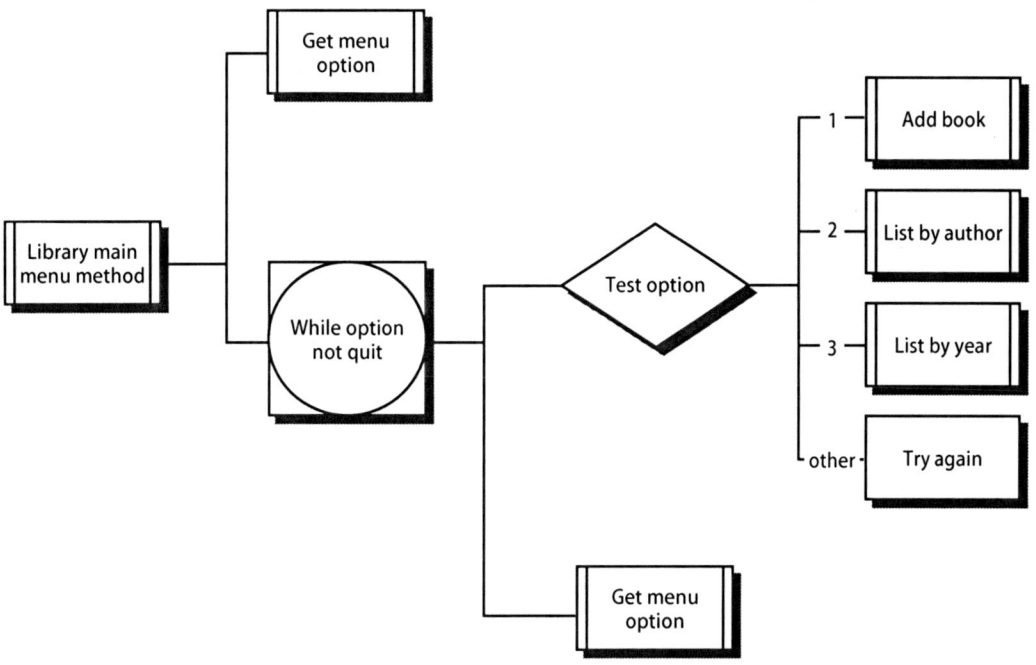

> **NOTE**
>
> By now, you should recognise the familiar read-ahead pattern here, which we should always use when designing with while loops.

Next, we'll design the menu method:

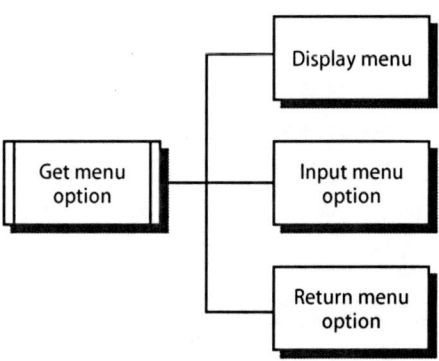

This is a very simple method: the menu is displayed to the user, an option is selected, and the value of the option is returned to the **main** method.

We will now design the methods that manipulate book objects, starting with adding a book to the collection:

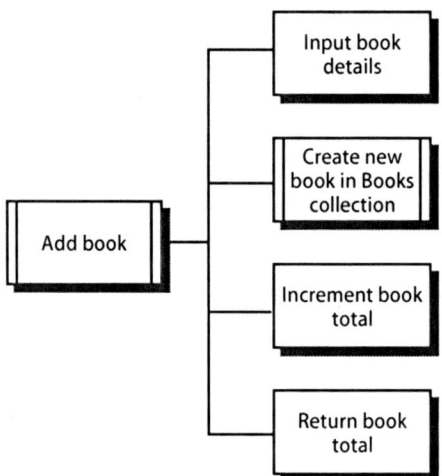

In this method, the user inputs the book's details (title, author and date). We will then call the **Book** class constructor which creates a new **Book** object. We also need to add one to the total number of books in the collection. This is important because when we search for books in the collection, we need to know how many objects to search for.

The final two methods in the program perform the searches, and the design of these shows how we use the total number of books in our search:

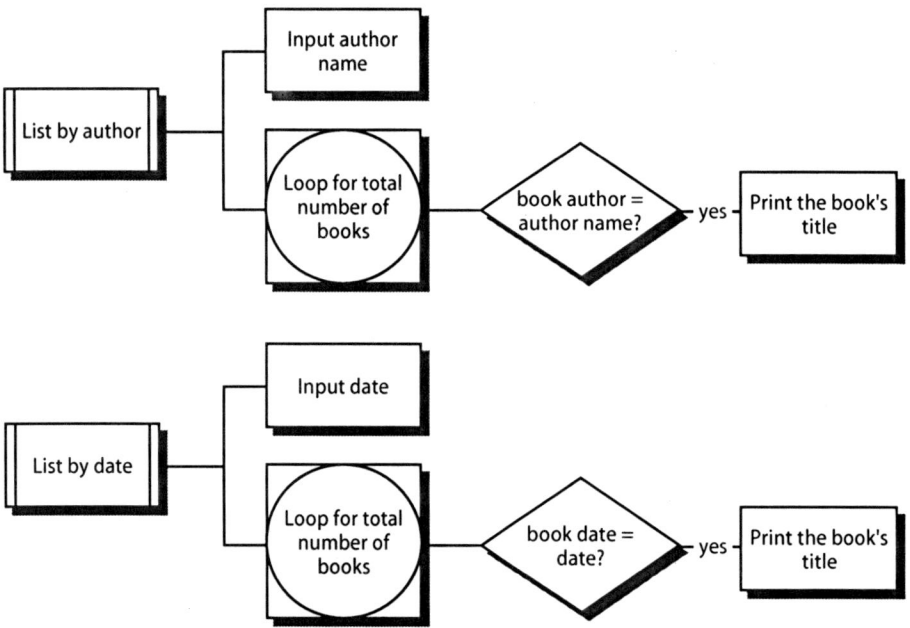

In each method, because we know how many times to loop (given to us by the total number of books updated whenever we add a new book), we will use a **for** loop to go through the book collection.

Now we've seen the designs, we will consider the Java code for each method, again starting with the main method:

```
public static void main(String[] args)
{
    Book books[] = new Book[100];
    int booksInLibrary = 0;
    int option;

    option = getMenuOpt();

    while (option != quit)
    {
        if (option == 1)
            booksInLibrary = addBook(books, booksInLibrary);
        else if (option == 2)
            listByAuthor(books, booksInLibrary);
        else if (option == 3)
            listByYear(books, booksInLibrary);
        else System.out.println("Invalid input - please try
        again");
        option = getMenuOpt();
    }
}
```

To clarify how the **main** method works, we will go through it carefully, line by line:

Firstly, we declare an array of **Book** objects:

```
Book books[] = new Book[100];
```

We have used an array here called **books**, and have reserved 100 spaces in the book collection. This would provide us with an absolute maximum of 100 book objects.

The next two lines define our other variables:

```
int booksInLibrary = 0;
```

```
int option;
```

WARNING

We need to initialise the **booksInLibrary** variable to zero, as we will be incrementing it every time we add another book. Remember that variables are not initialised for us in Java, so we have to do it explicitly ourselves when we need to.

You may have noticed already that there is no line to create a **Scanner** object to support user input. We actually don't need it in this program in the **main** method. Rather, all user input is done in the other methods, so that's where we will declare our **Scanner** objects.

The next line provides us with the opportunity to read the first menu option:

```
option = getMenuOpt();
```

The method that does this is called **getMenuOpt**. It returns to the **main** method the value selected by the user in the **getMenuOpt** method. The variable **option** stores this value. Next we test whether we can go into the loop:

```
while (option != quit)
```

Here we are testing the value selected by the user against something called **quit**, which is a constant value declared outside the **main** method. We will discuss this later, when we see the whole program, but for now, assume that the value of **quit** is zero – the option the user selects to end the program.

Of course, the user could quite legitimately have selected this option without bothering to do anything else.

> **REMEMBER**
>
> A while loop executes 0..n number of times. That's one of the reasons we use the read-ahead design.

Let's assume though, that the user selected a non-zero option. This will pass the test condition of the **while** loop, so we can enter the loop code. The value of **option** is tested, and we can call the appropriate method accordingly:

```
if (option == 1)
    booksInLibrary = addBook(books, booksInLibrary);
else if (option == 2)
    listByAuthor(books, booksInLibrary);
else if (option == 3)
    listByYear(books, booksInLibrary);
else System.out.println("Invalid input - try again");
```

We can now see a multi-way **if..else if...else** block of code. If the user selected option 1, the method **addBook** will be called. Selecting option 2 will call **listByAuthor**, and selecting option 3 calls **listByYear**. Any other selection will be invalid.

The **addBook** method returns the total number of books (**booksInLibrary**), as discussed when we designed the method. Notice that it takes two input parameters: **books** and **booksInLibrary**. In fact, you can see that ALL three methods take these as input parameters. **books** is the array of book objects. Each of the three methods require this information as they all require access to the books collection. Similarly, they all require knowledge of the number of books in the library. **addBook** needs this so it can add a new book in the array slot after the end of the collection, and **listByAuthor** and **listByYear** need it to know how many books to search through, as discussed when we designed those methods.

Finally, the **main** method, is to read the next value.

> **REMEMBER**
>
> We always do this as the very last line within a **while** loop.

```
option = getMenuOpt();
```

Now we will look at the code of each of the other methods, starting with **getMenuOpt**:

```
public static int getMenuOpt()
{
    Scanner menuOpt = new Scanner(System.in);
    int option;

    System.out.println("1. Add a book to the collection");
    System.out.println("2. List all books by author");
    System.out.println("3. List all books published in year");
    System.out.println(quit + ". Quit");

    option = menuOpt.nextInt();

    return option;
}
```

Hopefully, this method is self-explanatory. There are a couple of things to point out here though. Notice that our **Scanner** object is called **menuOpt**. So far, all of our programs have used a **Scanner** object called **input**. We used that name for convenience really, and to make life simple. However, there is no reason why we can't use any valid Java name for this. The other thing worth pointing out in this method is that we are again using the constant **quit**, this time purely to display its value in the menu (which is zero, of course).

Moving on, we'll now look at the code for the **addBook** method:

```
public static int addBook(Book bks[], int bookTot)
{
    Scanner input = new Scanner(System.in);
    String title;
    String aut;
    int yr;

    System.out.print("Enter book title ");
    title = input.nextLine();
    System.out.print("Enter author ");
    aut = input.nextLine();
    System.out.print("Enter publication date ");
    yr = input.nextInt();

    bks[bookTot] = new Book(title, aut, yr);

    bookTot++;

    return bookTot;
}
```

We won't go through every line in this method. Rather, we will pick out those which perhaps need further explanation. We will first look at the method declaration:

```
public static int addBook(Book bks[], int bookTot)
```

We can see that this method will return an **int** value. Looking at the input parameters, we can see that the first one, **bks** is an array. We know this because of the square brackets which immediately follow the parameter declaration. When we refer to the **bks** array within the method, we must provide an index inside those square brackets. Here is how it's done in the **addBook** method:

```
bks[bookTot] = new Book(title, aut, yr);
```

Here, the index is **bookTot**, which is always going to be the first empty space in the book collection. When there are no books in the collection **bookTot** is equal to zero, when there is one book, it will be equal to one, and so on. Remember that array indexing starts at zero, so the if there are *n* books in the collection, the next available space in the collection will be at array index *n*.

One other thing, notice that we use the **nextLine ()** method for inputting the book's title and author. This method supports multiple words being input into one **String** object. So, for example, the book's title could be *Great Expectations*, and the author could be *Charles Dickens*.

Everything else in the **addBook** method is straightforward, so we will now look at the **listByAuthor** method:

```
public static void listByAuthor(Book bks[], int bookTot)
{
    String name;
    Scanner input = new Scanner(System.in);

    System.out.print("Enter author's name ");
    name = input.nextLine();

    for (int count = 0; count < bookTot; count++)
    {
        if ( bks[count].getAuthor().equals(name) )
            System.out.println( bks[count].getTitle() );
    }

}
```

This method contains a **for** loop, as we specified in our design. We count from zero in the loop because we need to check from the first object in the book collection to the last object. The first one is at index zero, and the last one is at **bookTot** - 1. The **for** loop code we use here does exactly that, as the test (the second element in the loop statement) checks for **count** being LESS THAN **bookTot**.

The test within the loop checks whether the author name entered by the user is the same as that of the book object currently being scrutinised in the book collection.

Let's look at this more closely:

```
if ( bks[count].getAuthor().equals(name) )
```

At first sight, the test condition in this line of code may look very complicated, but if we analyse it in sections (each section being separated by a **dot**), things should appear simpler. Firstly, **bks[count]** uses the variable **count** as an index to each book object in the book collection. Every time we complete a cycle of the loop, **count** is incremented. This enables every book object to be tested in the collection. The next section **getAuthor ()** is the **accessor** method in the **Book** class which retrieves the author name of the book.

Finally, because the author name and the name input by the user are both **String** objects, we must use the **equals** method to test for equivalence.

The last method (**listByYear**) in the program is very similar to the **listByAuthor** method. You can see this by comparing the two design charts we did for these earlier. Here is the code:

```
public static void listByYear(Book bks[], int bookTot)
{
    Scanner input = new Scanner(System.in);
    int year;

    System.out.print("Enter year ");
    year = input.nextInt();

    for (int count = 0; count < bookTot; count++)
    {
        if ( bks[count].getDate() == year )
            System.out.println( bks[count].getTitle() );
    }

}
```

REMEMBER

Notice that the test condition in the **if** statement is different in this method. That's because we are testing an integer and not a string. Remember, we always use a double-equals when we are testing for equivalence between numerical values!

Now we have seen each method, we can glue them all together to make a whole program:

```
import java.util.Scanner;

/*
Design and write a program which enables a user to manage
books in a library.
The user will be presented with the following options in a
menu when the program runs.
The options available are:
    1. add a book to the collection. All books have a title,
    an author and a date of publication.
    2. list all books written by a particular author.
    3. list all books published in a given year
    0. quit the program

written by: Rich Picking
date: January 27th 2005

*/
/* The Book class */
class Book
```

```
{
    private String title;
    private String author;
    private int date;

    Book (String t, String a, int d)
    {
        title = t;
        author = a;
        date = d;
    }

    String getTitle()
    {
        return title;
    }

    String getAuthor()
    {
        return author;
    }

    int getDate()
    {
        return date;
    }
}
class Library
{
    static final int quit = 0;

    public static int getMenuOpt()
    {
        Scanner menuOpt = new Scanner(System.in);
        int option;

        System.out.println("1. Add a book to the
        collection");
        System.out.println("2. List all books by author");
        System.out.println("3. List all books published in
        year");
        System.out.println(quit + ". Quit");

        option = menuOpt.nextInt();
        return option;
    }

    public static int addBook(Book bks[], int bookTot)
    {
        Scanner input = new Scanner(System.in);
        String title;
        String aut;
```

```
        int yr;

        System.out.print("Enter book title ");
        title = input.nextLine();
        System.out.print("Enter author ");
        aut = input.nextLine();
        System.out.print("Enter publication date ");
        yr = input.nextInt();

        bks[bookTot] = new Book(title, aut, yr);

        bookTot++;

        return bookTot;
    }
    public static void listByAuthor(Book bks[], int bookTot)
    {
        String name;
        Scanner input = new Scanner(System.in);

        System.out.print("Enter author's name ");
        name = input.nextLine();

        for (int count = 0; count < bookTot; count++)
        {
            if ( bks[count].getAuthor().equals(name) )
                System.out.println( bks[count].getTitle() );
        }

    }
    public static void listByYear(Book bks[], int bookTot)
    {
        Scanner input = new Scanner(System.in);
        int year;

        System.out.print("Enter year ");
        year = input.nextInt();
        for (int count = 0; count < bookTot; count++)
        {
            if ( bks[count].getDate() == year )
                System.out.println( bks[count].getTitle() );
        }
    }

    public static void main(String[] args)
    {
        Book books[] = new Book[100];
        int booksInLibrary = 0;
        int option;
        option = getMenuOpt();

        while (option != quit)
        {
```

```
        if (option == 1)
            booksInLibrary = addBook(books, booksInLibrary);
        else if (option == 2)
            listByAuthor(books, booksInLibrary);
        else if (option == 3)
            listByYear(books, booksInLibrary);
        else System.out.println("Invalid input - try again");

        option = getMenuOpt();
    }
}
```

The only thing left to mention about this program is the constant **quit** which has cropped up in two of our methods. This constant is declared at the top of the **Library** class:

static final int quit = 0;

Because **quit** has been declared outside the methods within the class, it can be used by any of the methods in that class – in this case the **Library** class. When the code was written, it was considered a good idea to do this, as maybe at a later date, the value the user is expected to input to quit the program may be changed. If this is the case, the only place in the program where this needs to be done is in the line where **quit** is declared. This saves the potentially tricky task of finding every place in the program where the value is mentioned. Using constants in this way is generally regarded as good programming practice.

```
C:\Java>javac Library.java

C:\Java>java Library
1. Add a book to the collection
2. List all books by author
3. List all books published in year
0. Quit
1
Enter book title Great Expectations
Enter author Dickens
Enter publication date 1860
1. Add a book to the collection
2. List all books by author
3. List all books published in year
0. Quit
1
Enter book title Oliver Twist
Enter author Dickens
Enter publication date 1837
1. Add a book to the collection
2. List all books by author
3. List all books published in year
0. Quit
1
Enter book title The Mayor of Casterbridge
Enter author Hardy
Enter publication date 1886
1. Add a book to the collection
2. List all books by author
3. List all books published in year
0. Quit
2
Enter author's name Dickens
Great Expectations
Oliver Twist
1. Add a book to the collection
2. List all books by author
3. List all books published in year
0. Quit
0

C:\Java>
```

Exercise 8.4. Museum inventory

Here's a reminder of an exercise from earlier in this chapter: draw a class diagram and write the Java code to represent a vehicle museum. Vehicles have a licence plate, a year of manufacture, a value, and a colour. The museum has cars, which have a number of doors, seats, engine type (petrol or diesel), and engine size in litres. The museum also has motorbikes, which have a bike type (sports, tourer, or trails), and engine size in cubic centimetres (cc).

Using the knowledge you have gained since tackling this exercise, add the following features to the program in the form of a menu:

- add new vehicles (bikes or cars);
- list all vehicles manufactured in a given year;
- list all vehicles of 1 litre or more (1 litre = 1000cc);
- list all cars;
- list all bikes.

HINT: for the above two options, you can get a string representation of an object's class by calling the following method `getClass().toString()`, so to print object x's class, you would do this:

```
System.out.print( x.getClass().toString() );
```

Getting on with Java

Our Java *toolbox* now includes:

Structuring tools such as classes and methods which enable us to build programs in a **modular** way.

Control tools, such as loops, conditions and sequences, which enable us to control the *routes* our program code takes whilst it is running.

Data typing tools, such as integers, doubles, strings, and booleans, which enable us to work with different types of data. We can include classes, objects and arrays in this set of tools, as a more advanced and complex form of data.

Using these tools, you can design and build many, many useful programs. As you learn more Java, you will extend your toolset further and further. We have only seen the tip of the iceberg of this incredibly powerful language. To develop your knowledge further, you will need to read more advanced books, perhaps enrol on more advanced programming courses, and follow tutorials and other resources freely accessible on the Internet. A good place to start is to go to the creators of Java at **http://java.sun.com**. Here you will find literally thousands of pages on the language of Java and there are also many tutorials for you to follow.

This book has introduced some of the elementary principles of programming in general, and uses Java as its specific programming language. There are lots more languages in common use – just as there are spoken languages throughout the world. If you learn other languages, many of the principles you have encountered here will apply there too.

All programming languages support the principles of sequence, selection (conditions) and loops. Most of them support the concept of **modularity**, where you can break your programs down into smaller sub-programs (Java **methods**). Most also have their own rules for how data is manipulated.

Where you go from here is up to you. Perhaps you won't go any further with programming at all. Whatever you choose to do, hopefully you are a little curious about the possibilities of more advanced computer programming.

Java Forum

Post	How big is Java – how much more is there to know? ★
Reply	Java is a hugely powerful programming language which is one of the reasons why it is so popular. In this book, we have used a tiny subset of the language to help us learn the basics – just as if we were learning a new spoken language. Like a spoken language, Java is continually growing and evolving. New versions, new libraries and techniques are being developed by experts every day, all over the world. Most Java developments are available on the Internet, and there are many discussion groups and forums to support Java programmers – another reason why Java itself is so popular – the support available is second to none. To give you an idea of the wealth of information on Java, visit the official site at **http://java.sun.com**. Here, you can find up-to-date information, tutorials, forums, and the all-important class libraries, where you can expand on the small Java toolset presented here. The libraries (known as **API**, which stands for **application programming interface**), can be found at **http://java.sun.com/javase/reference/api.jsp**. As an introduction to this facility, why not try browsing through the Java classes for those you have come across already, such as **Scanner** and **System**. You will then find out how powerful they truly are. ☺

Post	I want to develop programs that save data – can Java do this? ★
Reply	A programming language isn't of much use if it doesn't allow us to save our work or data, and retrieve it at a later time. There are many ways to do this in Java, although it can be very complex – that's why it hasn't been considered in this introductory text. However, if you are interested, here is an example which uses the simplest way to do it – by using **files**.

In the code, there are several comments that explain what is going on:

```java
import java.util.*; /* need this library for file
handling */
import java.io.*;

/*
This program reads a set of names from a file. The user
can add to the names and write the new set to another
file.
*/

class NamesList
{
```

```java
public static void main(String[] args)
{
    /* the next two lines tell us the names of the
    files we are using in.txt is a text file which
    contains a list of single names on separate
    lines e.g.
        Fred
        Jane
        Bill
        Mary

    This program creates the file out.txt. If it
    already exists, it will be over-written.
    */
    File inFile = new File("in.txt");
    File outFile = new File("out.txt");

    Scanner input = new Scanner(System.in);

    /* create two objects - one for input, one for
    output */
    Scanner fileInput = null;
    PrintStream fileOutput = null;

    /* The next block of code uses the Java keywords
       'try' and 'catch'.
       They must be used when working with files.
       As long as the files open successfully, the
       code in the 'try' block runs. If there is a
       problem, the 'catch' code runs, to  catch the
       error. This prevents the program from
       crashing during execution.
       The technique is called 'exception handling'.
    */
    try
    {
        // point the i/o objects to the file objects

        fileInput = new Scanner(inFile);
        fileOutput = new PrintStream(outFile);
```

```
            }
            catch (FileNotFoundException e)
            {
                System.out.println ("File not found!");
                //Stop program if no file found
                System.exit (0);
            }

            // names will be held in an array called names
            String names[] = new String[100];
            int count = 0;
            int newNames;

            /* read the names from the input file into the
            array */
            while (fileInput.hasNext())
            {
                names[count] = fileInput.next();
                count++;
            }

            System.out.print
                ("How many new names would you like to add
                to the file? ");
            newNames = input.nextInt();

            // add the names to the array
            for (int i = 0; i < newNames; i++)
                names[count+i] = input.next();


            // now copy all the names to the output file
            for (int i = 0; i < newNames+count; i++)
                fileOutput.println(names[i]);

            // must close the files to finish!
            fileInput.close();
            fileOutput.close();
        }

    }
    ☺
```

Post	I want to know more about program design – where shall I go next? ⭐
Reply	In this book, we have used a graphical version of stepwise refinement. We also designed some class structures using a graphical method. There are many design and charting methods for developing computer programs. Arguably the best one for developing more advanced Java programs is called **UML** (**Unified Modelling Language**). There are many books and web sites on UML. A good starting point would be to visit **http://www.uml.org**, where you can read about the method, follow links to tutorials, and find software packages to help you use the notation.

Post	I want to program games and other graphical applications – how do I do that? ⭐
Reply	You can do this in Java. Java is especially good for developing graphical applications that run on the Internet. To do this, you will need to learn how to use Java classes that support graphics. You can learn all about how to do this from the official Java site. There are excellent tutorials available – visit **http://java.sun.com/docs/books/tutorial/index.html**. Writing graphical applications can be very complicated. Consequently, a number of specialist products (called **Interactive Development Environments** or **IDEs**) have been developed to help programmers build them.

As the briefest of introductions to writing applications that run on the Internet, here is an example. It is a very simple program, which runs inside a web browser. A Java program that runs inside a web browser is called an **applet**. Firstly, here is the code for the web page itself. Type this into a text editor and save it as **Applet.html**:

```
<html>
<applet code=ButtonApp.class>
</applet>
</html>
```

Now create the following Java program and save it as **ButtonApp.java**:

```
import java.awt.*;
import java.awt.event.*;
import java.applet.*;
/* This program generates a simple graphical interface
   where the user clicks a button to get a simple
   response */

public class ButtonApp extends Applet implements
ActionListener
```

```
{
    Button goButton; /* declared here so it can be used
    in both methods */

    /* this method runs when event happens i.e. the
    button is clicked */
    public void actionPerformed(ActionEvent e)
    {
        goButton.setLabel("OUCH!");
    }

    // init is an applet's version of the main method
    public void init()
    {
        goButton = new Button("CLICK ME");
        add(goButton);
        goButton.addActionListener(this);
    }
}
```

Compile the Java program in the usual way. Once this is done, rather than run the program from the command line, open up a web browser and open the **Applet. html** document. If all is well, you should see a graphical application in the web page which looks something like this:

Click the button in the web page, and the **actionPerformed** method automatically executes, giving you this:

Post	I want to learn another language – what is the next best step? ★
Reply	Perhaps the next step in your programming development is to take a look at some other languages. There are quite a few that are similar to Java in their rules and grammar. Such languages include **Javascript** (which is NOT the same as Java), **C++**, and **PHP**. They all derive from an older language known simply as **C**. Once you feel comfortable with your Java programming, any of these would be a good *next best step* to take. All these languages are particularly strong for certain applications, so maybe this will help you make your decision as to where to go next:

Javascript is excellent for developing engaging, interactive web pages;

C++ is excellent for developing games and other graphical applications;

PHP is excellent for creating dynamic web sites, such as e-commerce or e-learning applications.

Whatever you do next in developing your programming skills, remember to design you programs carefully, make sure you know how to solve the problem before you start coding, take your time during the coding phase, and always test your programs thoroughly!!

Above everything else, if you have enjoyed your first steps in programming, you will probably enjoy developing advanced programs even more. If you have found it difficult and frustrating however, be honest with yourself. Perhaps it would be best for you to develop your IT skills in other areas.

Appendix 1

SOLUTIONS TO SELECTED EXERCISES

Exercise 3.2: Age in 2050

 Design and build a program to input the year in which you were born and display the age you will be in the year 2050.

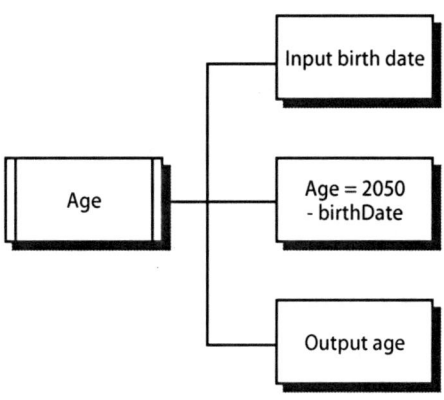

```
import java.util.Scanner;

/* This program enables the user to input the year in which
   they were born and displays their age in the year 2050 */
class Age
{
   public static void main (String [] args)
   {
       Scanner input = new Scanner(System.in);

       int yearBorn, age;

       System.out.print("Please input your year of birth ");

       yearBorn = input.nextInt();

       age = 2050 - yearBorn;

       System.out.print("In 2050, you will be " + age + "
       years old");
   }
}
```

Exercise 4.1: Capital city

 Design, write and test a program which asks the user to input the capital city of France. If they answer Paris, give them a congratulations message.

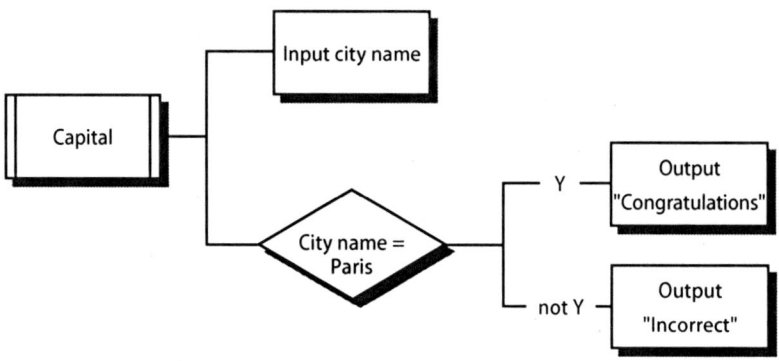

```
import java.util.Scanner;

// This program quizzes the user for the capital of France
class Capital
{
    public static void main (String [] args)
    {
        Scanner input = new Scanner(System.in);

        String cityName;

        System.out.print("Do you know the capital of France? ");

        cityName = input.next();

        if (cityName.equalsIgnoreCase("Paris"))
            System.out.print("Congratulations - you are
            right!");
        else
            System.out.print("Sorry, that is incorrect.")
    }
}
```

Exercise 4.4: Logic teaser

Below is a table. Columns 1 and 2 indicate two tests, A and B. As we know, tests always evaluate to true (T) and false (F). The rows of the table indicate combinations of the possible values for A and B. The other columns in the table show more complex tests which use A and B in various combinations along with conditional and logical operators. Fill out the rest of the table for each row, given the True/False values of A and B. To start you off, the first complex condition (A or B) has been completed.

A	B	A||B	A&&B	!(A||B)	!(A&&B)	!A||B	!(!A&&!B)	A||!B
T	T	T	T	F	F	T	T	T
T	F	T	F	F	T	F	T	T
F	T	T	F	F	T	T	T	F
F	F	F	F	T	T	T	F	T

Exercise 4.6: Insurance

Bike Direct insurance offers bike insurance as follows:

> basic rate = £30
> add £10 for a mountain bike
> add £5 for cyclists under 25.

 Design, write and test a program to input the type of bike – mountain or touring, and the cyclist's age, and calculate and display the premium payable.

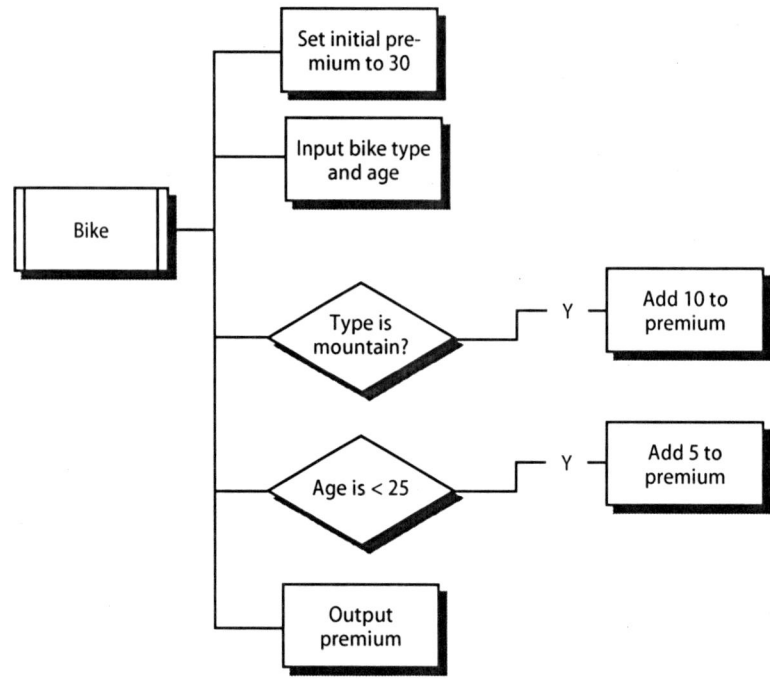

```
import java.util.Scanner;

/* Bike Direct insurance offers bike insurance as follows:

basic rate = £30
add £10 for a mountain bike
add £5 for cyclists under 25.

This program inputs the type of bike - mountain or touring,
and the cyclist's age, and calculate and display the premium
payable.
*/
class Bike
{
```

```
public static void main (String [] args)
{
    Scanner input = new Scanner(System.in);

    String type;
    int age;
    int premium = 30; /* set this to 30 - makes life
    simpler!! */

    System.out.print("Please input a the bike type: M or T ");
    type = input.next();

    System.out.print("Please input a the rider's age ");
    age = input.nextInt();

    // could easily use equalsIgnoreCase here instead!!
    if (type.equals("M") || type.equals("m"))
    {
        premium = premium + 10;
    }

    if (age < 25)
    {
        premium = premium + 5;
    }

    System.out.print("Premium payable is " + premium + "
    pounds");
    }
}
```

Exercise 5.4: Commission

 Design, write, and test a program to input the commission figures for ten sales staff; calculate and output the total commission overall and the average commission.

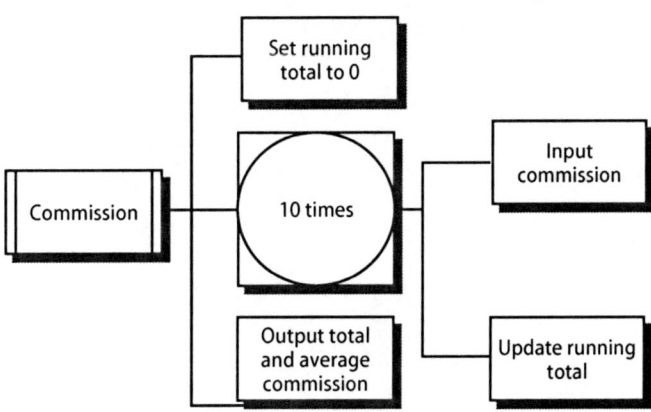

```
import java.util.Scanner;

/*
This program asks the user to input the commission figures
for ten sales staff; it then calculates and outputs the
total commission overall and the average commission.
*/
class Commission
{
    public static void main (String [] args)
    {
        Scanner input = new Scanner(System.in);

        int count;
        double com, total;

        total = 0; // must set this for a running total!!

        for (count = 1; count <= 10; count++)
        {
            System.out.print("Please input commission ");
            com = input.nextDouble();

            total = total + com;
        }

        System.out.println("Total sales: " + total + "
        pounds");
        System.out.print("Average sales: " + (total/10) + "
        pounds");
    }
}
```

Exercise 5.9: More student marks

Design, write and test a program to input student marks in a test. Output 'Pass' if the mark is 40 or above, otherwise output 'Fail'. Input a mark of -1 to finish the program.

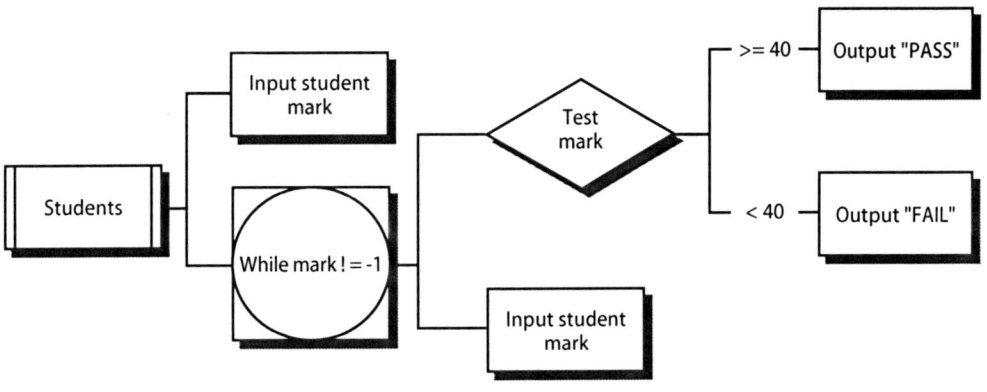

```java
import java.util.Scanner;

/*
This program asks the user to input student marks in a test.
Output 'Pass' if the mark is 40 or above, otherwise output
'Fail'.
Input a mark of -1 to finish the program.
*/
class Students
{
    public static void main (String [] args)
    {
        Scanner input = new Scanner(System.in);

        int mark;

        // READ AHEAD of the 'while' test!!!
        System.out.print("Please input mark (-1 to finish) ");
        mark = input.nextInt();

        while (mark != -1)
        {
            if (mark >= 40)
                    System.out.println("Pass");
            else
                    System.out.println("Fail");

            /* READ AHEAD of the 'while' test, otherwise you
            can't get out the loop!!! */
            System.out.print("Please input mark (-1 to finish) ");
            mark = input.nextInt();
        }

    }
}
```

Exercise 6.2: Circle area

 Design, build, and test a program that calculates the area of a circle, based on the user inputting its radius. You must write a separate method to calculate the formula: Area = $\pi r2$

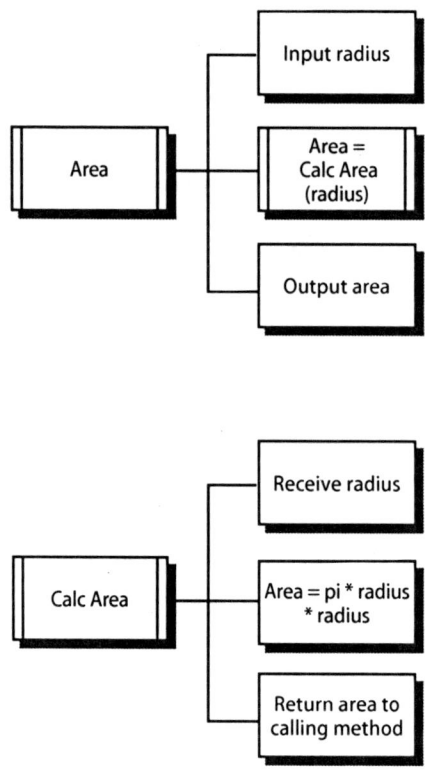

```java
import java.util.Scanner;

/*
This program calculates the area of a circle, based on the
user inputting its radius.
*/
class Area
{
    public static double calcArea (double rad)
    {
        // we can do this in a single line!!
        return (3.141 * rad * rad);
    }

    public static void main (String [] args)
    {
        Scanner input = new Scanner(System.in);
```

```
        double radius, circleArea;

        System.out.print("Please input the radius of the
        circle ");
        radius = input.nextDouble();

        circleArea = calcArea(radius);

        System.out.print("Area of the circle = " +
        circleArea);
    }
}
```

Exercise 7.1: Ice skaters

 Design and build a program to enable a user to input an array of six integers, which represent the scores allocated by judges in an ice skating competition. Once all scores have been entered into the array, use it to calculate and output the average score.

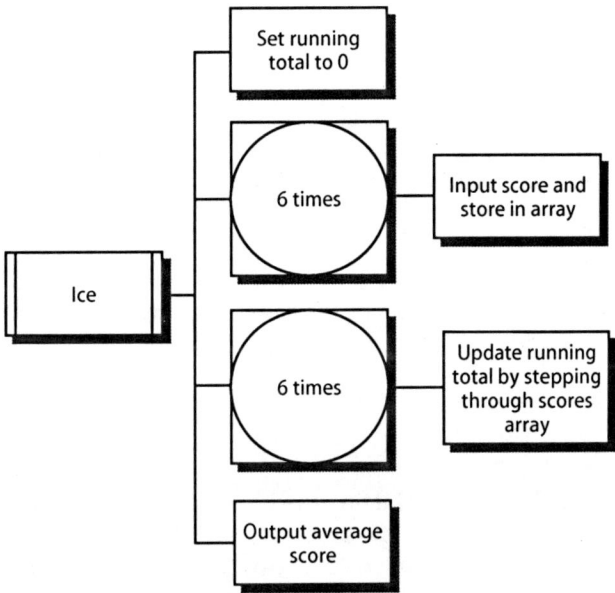

```java
import java.util.Scanner;

/*
This program enables a user to input an array of six
integers, which represent
the scores allocated by judges in an ice skating
competition.
Once all scores have been entered, it outputs the average
score.
*/
class Ice
{

    public static void main (String [] args)
    {
        Scanner input = new Scanner(System.in);

        int[] scores = new int[6];
        int count;
        int total = 0; // always initialise a totaliser!

        /* count from 0 to 5, to make the array processing
        easier */
        for (count = 0; count < 6; count++)
        {
            System.out.print("Please input the score for
            judge " + (count+1) + ": ");
            scores[count] = input.nextInt();
        }

        /* now all the scores are in, we can calculate the
        average by totalling them up, and dividing by 6 */
        for (count = 0; count < 6; count++)
        {
            total = total + scores[count];
        }

        // finally calculate and output the average.
        // we use 6.0 to force a fractional calculation,
        // otherwise Java will only give an integer result
        System.out.print("Average = " + (total/6.0) );
    }
}
```

Exercise 8.2: Music

 Draw a class diagram that describes what you know about three musical instruments. The instruments are piano, guitar, and violin. All of them have strings and all of them make a sound. Pianos have keys and violins have bows. You can strum a guitar and a violin, but you can't strum a piano – you have to hit the keys. Show some other properties and actions that can be performed with the instruments. To structure your class model, use a super class, called `Instrument`.

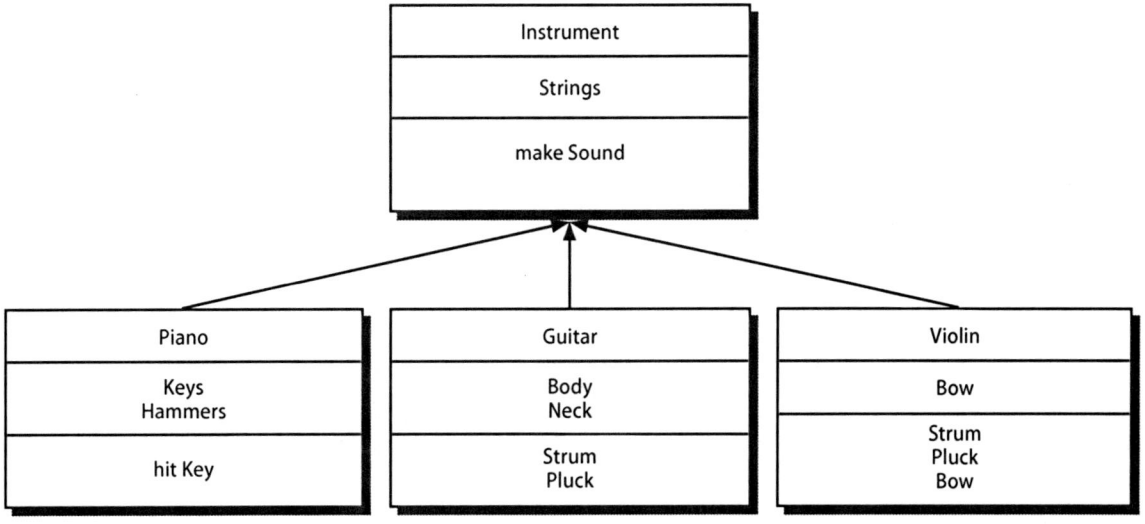

Appendix 2

COMMON ERRORS IN JAVA

The following screen shots show a number of very common mistakes made by new programmers in Java. The messages given by the compiler or the runtime environment are sometimes quite cryptic, so a little extra explanation is provided for each one.

Missing semi-colon at the end of a line

A very common mistake! The bug is indicated to be on line 15, although the missing semi-colon is always on the previous line. Count through the lines in your program, including empty ones to find where the problem is.

```
C:\WINDOWS\system32\cmd.exe
H:\JAVA>
H:\JAVA>
H:\JAVA>
H:\JAVA>
H:\JAVA>
H:\JAVA>
H:\JAVA>
H:\JAVA>
H:\JAVA>
H:\JAVA>
H:\JAVA>
H:\JAVA>
H:\JAVA>
H:\JAVA>
H:\JAVA>javac Students.java
Students.java:15: ';' expected

^
1 error

H:\JAVA>
H:\JAVA>
```

Wrong class or file name

Remember to make sure the file name and the class name are the same. If they aren't, the program may compile, but you will get an error when you try to run it, as shown in the example below:

```
C:\WINDOWS\system32\cmd.exe
H:\JAVA>
H:\JAVA>
H:\JAVA>
H:\JAVA>
H:\JAVA>
H:\JAVA>
H:\JAVA>
H:\JAVA>
H:\JAVA>
H:\JAVA>
H:\JAVA>
H:\JAVA>javac Students.java

H:\JAVA>java Students
Exception in thread "main" java.lang.NoClassDefFoundError: Students

H:\JAVA>
H:\JAVA>
```

Wrong class or file name 2

In this example, the file name is correct, but when the program is set to run, the programmer has used the wrong case for the class name. A very common mistake!

```
C:\WINDOWS\system32\cmd.exe
H:\JAVA>
H:\JAVA>
H:\JAVA>
H:\JAVA>
H:\JAVA>
H:\JAVA>
H:\JAVA>javac Students.java

H:\JAVA>java students
Exception in thread "main" java.lang.NoClassDefFoundError: students (wrong
  Students)
        at java.lang.ClassLoader.defineClass1(Native Method)
        at java.lang.ClassLoader.defineClass(Unknown Source)
        at java.security.SecureClassLoader.defineClass(Unknown Source)
        at java.net.URLClassLoader.defineClass(Unknown Source)
        at java.net.URLClassLoader.access$100(Unknown Source)
        at java.net.URLClassLoader$1.run(Unknown Source)
        at java.security.AccessController.doPrivileged(Native Method)
        at java.net.URLClassLoader.findClass(Unknown Source)
        at java.lang.ClassLoader.loadClass(Unknown Source)
        at sun.misc.Launcher$AppClassLoader.loadClass(Unknown Source)
        at java.lang.ClassLoader.loadClass(Unknown Source)
        at java.lang.ClassLoader.loadClassInternal(Unknown Source)

H:\JAVA>
```

Missing brackets

In the next example, the programmer has forgotten the two round brackets that are missing after the **nextInt** method is called. The compiler has taken us straight to the problem, on line 18.

```
C:\WINDOWS\system32\cmd.exe

H:\JAVA>
H:\JAVA>
H:\JAVA>
H:\JAVA>
H:\JAVA>
H:\JAVA>
H:\JAVA>
H:\JAVA>
H:\JAVA>
H:\JAVA>
H:\JAVA>
H:\JAVA>
H:\JAVA>javac Students.java
Students.java:18: cannot find symbol
symbol  : variable nextInt
location: class java.util.Scanner
        mark = input.nextInt;
                         ^
1 error

H:\JAVA>
H:\JAVA>
H:\JAVA>
H:\JAVA>
H:\JAVA>
```

Stuck loop

Remember that there is no semi-colon after a **while**, **for**, or **if** statement. Strange things can happen when a seemingly working program hits the problem while it is running. In the example below, the programmer has typed a semi-colon after a **while** statement, causing the program to enter a never-ending loop.

```
C:\WINDOWS\system32\cmd.exe

H:\JAVA>
H:\JAVA>
H:\JAVA>
H:\JAVA>
H:\JAVA>
H:\JAVA>
H:\JAVA>
H:\JAVA>
H:\JAVA>
H:\JAVA>
H:\JAVA>
H:\JAVA>
H:\JAVA>
H:\JAVA>
H:\JAVA>
H:\JAVA>
H:\JAVA>
H:\JAVA>javac Students.java

H:\JAVA>java Students
Please input mark (-1 to finish) 30
```

175

Stuck loop 2

Here is another example of a never-ending loop. The program is going round and round for ever, because the programmer forgot to put in the read-ahead code towards the end of a **while** loop.

```
C:\WINDOWS\system32\cmd.exe
Fail
Fail
Fail
Fail
Fail
Fail
Fail
Fail
Fail
Fail
Fail
Fail
Fail
Fail
Fail
Fail
Fail
Fail
Fail
Fail
Fail
Fail
Fail
```

Missing curly bracket

The consequences of missing a single open curly bracket – in this case at the beginning of a program – may look serious. Many errors are generated because the compiler can't work out where the program begins. Remember to use neat indentation, and any errors of this sort should be easier to spot.

```
C:\WINDOWS\system32\cmd.exe
H:\JAVA>
H:\JAVA>
H:\JAVA>javac Students.java
Students.java:11: ';' expected

^
Students.java:17: <identifier> expected
        System.out.print("Please input mark (-1 to finish) ");
                                              ^
Students.java:18: <identifier> expected
        mark = input.nextInt();
             ^
Students.java:20: illegal start of type
                while (mark != -1)
                     ^
Students.java:31: <identifier> expected
^
Students.java:33: 'class' or 'interface' expected
}
^
Students.java:34: 'class' or 'interface' expected
^
7 errors

H:\JAVA>
```

Missing curly bracket 2

In this example, a close bracket is missing. The compiler has done a better job of locating the error though.

```
C:\WINDOWS\system32\cmd.exe

H:\JAVA>
H:\JAVA>
H:\JAVA>
H:\JAVA>
H:\JAVA>
H:\JAVA>
H:\JAVA>
H:\JAVA>
H:\JAVA>
H:\JAVA>
H:\JAVA>
H:\JAVA>
H:\JAVA>javac Students.java
Students.java:34: '}' expected
^
1 error

H:\JAVA>
H:\JAVA>
H:\JAVA>
H:\JAVA>
H:\JAVA>
H:\JAVA>
H:\JAVA>
H:\JAVA>
```

Missing brackets in an if statement

An easy mistake to make, but the compiler has given us a relatively helpful message.

```
C:\WINDOWS\system32\cmd.exe

H:\JAVA>
H:\JAVA>
H:\JAVA>
H:\JAVA>
H:\JAVA>
H:\JAVA>
H:\JAVA>
H:\JAVA>
H:\JAVA>
H:\JAVA>
H:\JAVA>
H:\JAVA>
H:\JAVA>javac Students.java
Students.java:22: '(' expected
                if mark >= 40
                  ^
Students.java:23: illegal start of expression
                    System.out.println("Pass");
                                              ^
2 errors

H:\JAVA>
H:\JAVA>
H:\JAVA>
H:\JAVA>
H:\JAVA>
```

Forgot to import the class library

Another easy-to-make mistake. The programmer has omitted the **import** statement at the top of the program. Consequently, the **Scanner** class is unknown to the program. Always use a program template to overcome the chances of this happening.

```
C:\WINDOWS\system32\cmd.exe
H:\JAVA>
H:\JAVA>
H:\JAVA>
H:\JAVA>
H:\JAVA>javac Students.java
Students.java:12: cannot find symbol
symbol  : class Scanner
location: class Students
                Scanner input = new Scanner(System.in);
                ^
Students.java:12: cannot find symbol
symbol  : class Scanner
location: class Students
                Scanner input = new Scanner(System.in);
                                    ^
2 errors

H:\JAVA>
H:\JAVA>
H:\JAVA>
H:\JAVA>
H:\JAVA>
H:\JAVA>
H:\JAVA>
H:\JAVA>
```

Forgot to declare a variable

In this example, the programmer forgot to declare a variable called **mark**. Every time the variable is used in the program, an error will be generated.

```
C:\WINDOWS\system32\cmd.exe
H:\JAVA>
H:\JAVA>javac Students.java
Students.java:18: cannot find symbol
symbol  : variable mark
location: class Students
        mark = input.nextInt();
        ^
Students.java:20: cannot find symbol
symbol  : variable mark
location: class Students
                while (mark != -1)
                       ^
Students.java:22: cannot find symbol
symbol  : variable mark
location: class Students
                if (mark >= 40)
                    ^
Students.java:29: cannot find symbol
symbol  : variable mark
location: class Students
                mark = input.nextInt();
                ^
4 errors

H:\JAVA>
```

INDEX

Also from Lexden Publishing:

Title	Author	ISBN
Computer Systems Architecture	R Newman, E Gaura, D Hibbs	978-1-903337-07-0
Computer Networks (2nd Edition)	P Irving	978-1904995-08-X
Databases	R Warrender	978-1-903337-08-0
Get On Up With Java	R Picking	978-1904995-18-0
JavaScript: Creating Dynamic Web Pages	E Gandy, S Stobart	978-1904995-07-4
Multimedia Computing	D Cunliffe, G Elliott	978-1904995-05-0
User Interface Design	J Le Peuple, R Scane	978-1-903337-19-6
Visual Programming	D Leigh	978-1-903337-11-0
Website Management	G Elliott	978-1904995-21-0
Access 2002: An Advanced Course for Students	S Coles, J Rowley	978-1904995-06-7
Access 2000: An Introductory Course for Students	S Coles, J Rowley	978-1-903300-14-5
Access 2000: An Advanced Course for Students	S Coles, J Rowley	978-1-903300-15-2
Excel 2002: An Advanced Course for Students	J Muir	978-1-84445-005-3
Excel 2000: An Introductory Course for Students	J Muir	978-1-903300-16-9
Excel 2000: An Advanced Course for Students	J Muir	978-1-903300-17-6
Word 2000: An Introductory Course for Students	S Coles, J Rowley	978-1-903300-18-3
Word 2000: An Advanced Course for Students	S Coles, J Rowley	978-1-903300-19-0
The Small Book of Big Presentation Skills	R. K. Bali, A. Dwivedi	978-1-904995-17-3
Key Skills Level 1: Information and Communication Technology	R Whitley Willis, M Kench	978-1-904995-27-2
Key Skills Level 2: Information and Communication Technology	R Whitley Willis, M Kench	978-1-904995-26-5
Key Skills Level 1: Communication; Application of Number; Information and Communication Technology	R Whitley Willis, L Gabrielle	978-1904995-10-1
Key Skills Level 2: Communication; Application of Number; Information and Communication Technology	R Whitley Willis, L Gabrielle	978-1904995-17-9

To order, please call our order hotline on 01202 712909 or visit our website at **www.lexden-publishing.co.uk** for further information.

Printed in the United Kingdom
by Lightning Source UK Ltd.
122758UK00001B/97-142/A